Extraordinary Jobs in the

FOOD INDUSTRY

Also in the Extraordinary Jobs series:

Extraordinary Jobs in the

FOOD INDUSTRY

ALECIA T. DEVANTIER & CAROL A. TURKINGTON

Ferguson

An imprint of Infobase Publishing

Extraordinary Jobs in the Food Industry

Copyright © 2006 by Alecia T. Devantier and Carol A. Turkington

Ferguson
An imprint of Infobase Publishing
132 West 31st Street
New York NY 10001

Library of Congress Cataloging-in-Publication Data

Devantier, Alecia T.
  Extraordinary jobs in the food industry / Alecia T. Devantier and Carol A. Turkington.
    p. cm.
  Includes index.
  ISBN 0-8160-5856-3 (alk. paper)
  1. Food service—Vocational guidance. I. Turkington, Carol. II. Title.
  TX911.3.V62D48 2006
  647.95023—dc22   2005036748

Ferguson books are available at special discounts when purchased in bulk quantities for businesses, associations, institutions, or sales promotions. Please call our Special Sales Department in New York at (212) 967-8800 or (800) 322-8755.

You can find Ferguson on the World Wide Web at http://www.fergpubco.com

Text design by Mary Susan Ryan-Flynn
Cover design by Salvatore Luongo

Printed in the United States of America

VB FOF 10 9 8 7 6 5 4 3 2 1

This book is printed on acid-free paper.

CONTENTS

ACKNOWLEDGMENTS

This book wouldn't have been possible without the help of countless others who referred us to individuals to interview and came up with information about a wide variety of odd and unusual jobs. We deeply appreciate the time and generosity of all those foodies who took the time to talk to us about their unusual jobs in the food business. Thanks also to all the people who helped with interviews and information and the production of this book, including Susan Shelly McGovern and Barbara Turkington.

Thanks also to our editors James Chambers and Sarah Fogarty, to Vanessa Nittoli, to our agents Ed Claflin of Ed Claflin Literary Associates and Gene Brissie of James Peter Associates, and to Michael and Kara.

ARE YOU CUT OUT FOR A CAREER IN THE FOOD INDUSTRY?

Just for fun sometime, click onto your favorite Internet search engine and type in one word: *food*. A Google search on that word came up with about 271 million results. Just for the sake of comparison, a Google search on *U.S. presidents* turned up 53 million results, *Civil War* produced about 39 million, and *God* resulted in 67 million sites.

That just shows you that the massive amount of information available out there concerning food sends a clear message: It may be love that makes the world go round, but when it comes to what's most important to us, food is right up there. If you're considering a career in the food industry, you've got thousands of choices. The food industry employs millions of Americans, and millions more are employed in jobs that are somehow related to food. Before it ends up in your hands, food is manufactured, processed, inspected, prepared, packaged, and marketed—forming the basis for a huge food industry. While this book profiles a number of unusual food industry jobs, it doesn't even scratch the surface of the food-related jobs that exist and are available.

Most of us enjoy going to a nice restaurant for dinner. Clean cloth napkins, sparkling water glasses, carefully prepared and served food, and attentive service combine to make a for a memorable dining experience. Think for a moment about how many people it takes to make that dinner happen. Food-related jobs!

Then take a minute and think about that cereal you had for breakfast this morning. How many different types of jobs do you think it takes to get a box of cereal on the shelf of your local grocery store? Start with the farmer who plants the wheat or oat seeds, and then see how many other jobs you can think of that are necessary for cereal production. More food-related jobs!

Of course, the word *food* relates to far more than what's on your plate when you sit down for dinner. Aspects of food are intertwined with health, politics, advertising, education, religion, family, the economy, law, oil production, transportation, and the infrastructure of the country.

In the United States, food is more than a source of nourishment. The past 40 years have seen an explosion in the food industry at nearly all levels. We eat out more often than ever before. The Food Network exists solely to provide all types of food-related shows.

Food is everywhere, dispensed from machines, by street vendors, and in snack bars, fast food restaurants, diners, and fine-dining establishments.

Some kids like to tinker with cars. Other kids spend hours in front of their computers, figuring out ingenious ways to improve their online surfing. Still others love the outdoors, or music, or painting. But then there are some kids who just seem to be born interested in food. You know who you are—you can't wait to whip up a new version of *mousse au chocolat* or figure out how to make that latest batch of popcorn taste really good. Maybe you're fascinated with creating interesting ways to combine ingredients, or you can't imagine a more fun thing to do than figure out how to bottle wine or mix up some malt and yeast and end up with beer.

When you think about your future career, would you rather create a new type of *vol au vent* than write up a company report? Would you rather design a hand-made ice sculpture than a new type of aircraft? Sculpt a life-size cow out of butter rather than pound out 45 pages of financial reviews? Let's face it—some folks are made for working with food and beverages. They're made for wearing a chef's toque, not a Burberry's tweed suit, and they'll never fit inside a normal 9-to-5 time slot.

And that's okay.

Take some time to think about the kind of person you are and the sorts of experiences you dream of having. Are you passionate about food, ingredients, cooking, brewing, or beverages? If you take the time to follow your heart—along with your nose, your palate, and your stomach—you'll end up doing what you love to do.

Of course, loving what you do is only part of having a successful career in food. You've got to be willing to work hard. Do you relish working incredibly long hours to produce something really fine? If you're thinking about a career in food, you'd better be, because many of these jobs require incredible dedication and very long hours. Some kids have the idea that they'll spend four years in college, graduate, and find the world just waiting on their doorstep, chef's apron in hand. But unless you're related to Julia Child or James Beard, it may not be that easy.

Then there are the stumbling blocks placed in your path not by your own reluctance, but by the reservations of others. Have you inherited a lot of "shoulds" in thinking about the kind of person you want to be? These *shoulds* inside your head can be a major stumbling block in finding and enjoying an unusual job in the food industry. Remember, if you're born with a dream, you owe it to yourself to go after it, no matter how unusual, odd, weird, or just plain batty it may seem to others. Can you imagine what chef Jacques Perrier's *maman* said when he told her he wanted to cook for the rest of his life?

You'll also need to realize that there may be other people who aren't so happy with your career choice. You may hear complaints from your family and friends who just can't understand why you don't want a job with more "regular" hours. And certainly, if your food urges take you into the restaurant business, the failure rate for these new ventures can be depressingly high. If you confide your career dreams to some people, you may find they try to discourage you. Can you handle their continuous skepticism?

Think about these things carefully, but don't cheat yourself. You're going to grow older, so you might as well live your life doing what you love to do.

Living and working in the food business isn't necessarily an easy career. You'll work hard—very hard. But if you allow yourself to explore the options that are out there, you'll find that work and play often tend to become the same thing. Push past your doubts and fears and let your journey begin!

Carol A. Turkington
Alecia T. Devantier

HOW TO USE THIS BOOK

Students face a lot of pressure to decide what they want to be when they grow up. Some kids have discovered their passion right from the beginning: Some just love to work outdoors, digging in gardens or working with animals. Others are fascinated with science, with mathematics, or with languages. But what about those kids who just love everything to do with food, cooking, and preparing a meal? Where can you go to find out answers you might have about these exciting, creative, nontraditional jobs in the food industry?

For example, where can you go to find out how to become a brewmaster, an ice sculptor, or a turkey talk-line expert? What does it take to become a butter sculptor or a winemaker? Is it really possible to make a living as a movie set caterer?

Look no further! This book will take you inside the world of a number of different culinary jobs, answering all sorts of questions you might have, letting you know what to expect if you pursue that career, introducing you to someone making a living that way, and providing resources if you want to do further research.

THE JOB PROFILES

All job profiles in this book have been broken down into the following fact-filled sections: At a Glance, Overview, and Interview. Each offers a distinct perspective on the job, and taken together give you a full view of the job in question.

At a Glance

Each entry starts out with an At a Glance box, offering a snapshot of important basic information to give you a quick glimpse of that particular job, including salary, education/experience, requirements, personal attributes, and outlook.

- *Salary range.* What can you expect to make? Salary ranges for the jobs in this book are as accurate as possible; many are based on the U.S. Bureau of Labor statistics' *Occupational Outlook Handbook*. Information also comes from individuals, actual job ads, employers, and experts in that field. It's important to remember that salaries for any particular job vary greatly depending on experience, geographic location, and level of education.
- *Education/Experience.* What kind of education or experience does the job require? This section will give you some information about the types of education or experience requirements the job might call for.
- *Personal attributes.* Do you have what it takes to do this job? How do you think of yourself? How would someone else describe you? This section will give you an idea of some of the personality characteristics and traits that might be useful to you if you choose this career. These attributes were collected from articles written about the job, as well as recommendations from employers and people actually doing the jobs, working in the field.

✔ *Requirements.* Are you qualified? You might as well make sure you meet any health, medical, or screening requirements before going any further with your job pursuit.

✔ *Outlook.* What are your chances of finding a job in the food business? This section is based in part on the *Occupational Outlook Handbook,* as well as on interviews with employers and experts. This information is typically a "best guess" based on the information that's available right now, including changes in the economy, situations in the United States and around the world, job trends, and retirement levels. These and many other factors can influence changes in the availability of jobs in the food business.

Overview

This section will give you an idea of what to expect from the job. For most of these unusual jobs, there really is no such thing as an average day. Each day is a whole new adventure, bringing with it a unique set of challenges and rewards. This section will give you an idea of what a person in this position might expect on a day-to-day basis.

The overview also gives you more details about how to get into the profession, offering a more detailed look at the required training or education, if needed, and providing an in-depth look at what to expect during that training or educational period.

No job is perfect, and **Pitfalls** takes a look at some of the obvious and maybe not-so-obvious pitfalls of the job. Don't let the pitfalls discourage you from pursuing a career; they are just things to be aware of while making your decision.

For many people, loving their job so much that they look forward to going to work every day is enough of a perk. **Perks** looks at some of the other perks of the job you may not have considered.

What can you do now to start working toward the career of your dreams? **Get a Jump on the Job** will give you some ideas and suggestions for things that you can do now, even before graduating from high school, to start preparing for this job. Opportunities include training programs, internships, groups and organizations to join, as well as practical skills to learn.

Interview

In addition to taking a general look at the job, each entry features a discussion with someone who is lucky enough to do this job for a living. In addition to giving you an inside look at the job, this interview provides valuable tips for anyone interested in pursuing a career in the same field.

APPENDIXES

Appendix A (Associations, Organizations, and Web Sites) lists of places to look for additional information about each specific job, including professional associations, societies, unions, government organizations, training programs, forums, official government links, and periodicals. Associations and other groups are a great source of information, and there's an association for just about every job you can imagine. Many groups and associations have a student membership level, which you can join by paying a small fee. There are many advantages to joining an association, including the chance to make important contacts, receive helpful newsletters, and attend workshops or conferences. Some associations also offer scholarships that will make it easier to further your education.

In **Appendix B** (**Online Career Resources**) we've gathered some of the best general Web sites about unusual jobs in the food industry, along with a host of very specific Web sites tailored to individual food-related jobs. Use these as a springboard to your own Internet research. Of course, all of this information is current as we've written this book, but Web site addresses do change. If you can't find what you're looking for at a given address, do a simple Internet search—the page may have been moved to a different location.

In **Appendix C** (**Culinary Schools**) we've gathered the names and addresses of some of the country's top culinary schools, along with brief descriptions of the courses and degrees available. Web site addresses are provided where available.

READ MORE ABOUT IT

In this back-of-the-book listing, we've gathered some helpful books that can give you more detailed information about each job we discuss in this book. Find these at the library or bookstore if you want to learn even more about jobs in the food industry.

BENIHANA CHEF

OVERVIEW

When you're a chef at a Benihana restaurant, you're expected to do more than just cook steak, seafood, chicken, and vegetables. Benihana chefs are performers, whose theatrical abilities are just as important as their culinary expertise.

The Benihana chain was founded about 40 years ago in New York City by Hiroak Aoki, the son of a popular Japanese entertainer. Company literature claims that since the opening of the first restaurant, Benihana chefs have provided the "longest-running dinner show in the world." When the first Benihana restaurant opened in 1964, Americans were largely unfamiliar with Japanese food, and tableside cooking was virtually unknown. The restaurant chain is often credited with introducing the American public to both Japanese cuisine and tableside dining. The original four-table restaurant has grown to a chain of more than 80 U.S. facilities, with locations in Canada, South America, Asia, Europe, and Australia. This means good chefs are always in demand.

You can't just walk in off the street, however, and expect to fire up the *teppan-yaki* tables (the large hibachi grills used for Benihana's signature tableside cooking). It takes about six months of training to become a Benihana chef. Potential chefs used to be sent to a central training facility in New Orleans to learn the tricks of the business. These days, however, they're trained on-site in restaurants across the country. Traditionally, Benihana chefs have been men, and most still are. However,

AT A GLANCE

Salary Range
About $6 to $7 an hour, plus tips, to start. An executive chef who has been with the company for many years, however, can expect to make between $50,000 and $80,000, according to a spokesperson for the restaurant chain.

Education/Experience
There are no specific educational requirements for Benihana chefs, although some culinary training is beneficial. All chefs, regardless of prior education and experience, are trained in Benihana kitchens.

Personal Attributes
You must be outgoing and personable, and able to keep up a running conversation with customers while working with sharp knives and hot grills. Good hand-eye coordination is a must. You should be neat in appearance and able to make diners feel comfortable.

Requirements
Benihana chefs are expected to interact with customers; they must be able to speak the same language as most patrons.

Outlook
With more than 80 restaurants in the United States and additional ones under construction or in the planning stages, the demand for Benihana chefs should continue to increase in the foreseeable future.

women are now accepted for training, and some are currently employed as chefs.

The job of a Benihana chef is to prepare a great meal for customers while keeping them entertained. Appropriately attired in crisp white chef's clothing, the star of the show arrives at his or her station with a cart full of food and

Oscar Aviles, Benihana chef

A typical work day for Benihana chef Oscar Aviles might include cooking for a celebrity such as singer Gloria Estefan, basketball star Shaquille O'Neal, or Latin singer/songwriter Jon Secada. But regardless of who shows up for dinner, Aviles is constantly ready to perform.

"If you want to be a Benihana chef, you have to really be into it," says Aviles, a native of Nicaragua. "You can't be afraid to cook right in front of your customers. You need a good sense a humor and a good personality. You have to be in a good mood all of the time."

Aviles, who has been a chef with Benihana for more than 14 years, got his training on site, starting as a kitchen helper. All the food that the chefs cook in front of their customers is prepped in the kitchen. The tricks, such as spinning knives and tossing food so that it lands in a precise location on the sizzling grill, come after the basics have been mastered.

"The first thing is to learn how to prepare everything in the kitchen," Aviles says. "Once you learn how to prepare all of the meals and side dishes, the chief chef will teach you how to cook the food and do all of the tricks."

The chef-in-training gets lessons on cooking on the teppanyaki tables between lunch and dinner when the restaurant is empty. It is then, Aviles says, that the chief chef shares tips and secrets, passing along the Benihana traditions. "That's how you learn," Aviles says. "And while you're learning, the chief chef eats whatever you cook, so you want it to be good."

Aviles' favorite dish to prepare in front of his customers is the Hibachi Chateaubriand, which is beef tenderloin served with garlic butter. "It is very tender and the best cut of steak," Aviles says. "It melts in your mouth when you add the garlic butter."

Benihana chefs work normal shifts and have scheduled days off, so the schedule isn't too intimidating. Aviles says that he enjoys his work immensely, and particularly likes interacting with his customers. "As a Benihana chef, I get to make a lot of people happy," Aviles says. "They always have fun when they eat at my table."

condiments that will be used in preparing the meal. While each chef has his or her own tricks and techniques, there are some popular Benihana moves common to all the restaurants. These might include tossing eggs in the air and cracking them with knives as they fall toward the grill, using knives to launch food from the grill directly onto the plates of diners, and slicing shrimp lengthwise so that they fan out onto the grill. Sharpening knives in a dramatic fashion is also a hallmark technique for a Benihana chef.

Prospective chefs only learn these flashy techniques after they've been well trained in the basics of preparing all the food necessary for cooking. A lot of preparation work occurs in the kitchen, out of sight of the customers. Benihana management insists that its chefs learn the craft from the ground up, working first in the kitchen and then moving to the dining room.

Pitfalls

While the work is enjoyable and fun, it can be a demanding task to be constantly cheerful and happy, even when you're not feeling that way. Also, until you're established and have some experience under your belt, the pay can be pretty low.

Perks

If you like to cook and be the center of attention, Benihana chef might just be your perfect job. Plus, once you've established yourself and have the position of head chef, you can make a good salary. Benihana restaurants are located all over the world. If you're interested in traveling, you may be able to relocate from restaurant to restaurant.

Get a Jump on the Job

Visit a Benihana restaurant and watch the chefs at work. If there's no Benihana in your area, there may be another Japanese restaurant near you that offers a similar cooking presentation. Read up on Japanese cooking and the rituals associated with preparing food. Learn basic culinary skills and practice cooking as much as possible.

BREWMASTER

OVERVIEW

Just like the making of fine wine, the production of a specialty craft beer is a complex process involving detailed recipes, an understanding of yeasts and the fermentation process, and a precise balance of ingredients. What you end up with is a unique-tasting full-bodied beer, far different from a commercial mass-produced brew. Craft beer is an all-malt beverage made in small batches for local customers, by any one of America's small, regional, micro-, or pub-breweries. The focus is on distinctive taste and aroma, achieved by using the best ingredients.

The inspiration for brewing craft beers can be traced to British, German, or Belgian traditions, and range from pale to dark colors and from mild to strong alcohol content. Compared with other beers, their emphasis is more on flavor, and less on appealing to a mass market.

When America's small brewers first produced beer in small batches, it was called microbrewed beer, because it was produced by a microbrewery—a brewery or brewpub producing less than 15,000 barrels a year. But as dozens of high-quality microbreweries became successful, they got much bigger yet still kept on brewing excellent, full-flavored specialty beers.

Today, those beers are called craft beers, produced by all sizes of breweries. This name helps differentiate between the more commercial American beer made with rice, corn, and sugar adjuncts, and the fuller American craft beer made with malt.

Craft brewmasters use a traditional process to create their products, blending hop flowers and water with the sugars from malted grains such as barley or wheat. It's the brewmaster's skill that brings out the desired aroma, color, foam, and flavor of the hops and malt by using specific recipes. Craft beer isn't usually pasteurized, but it does go through a filtration process to improve clarity. After careful temperature-controlled aging, the beer is packaged and ready for sale. To get from grains to bottle, ale takes about two weeks and lagers take about five weeks.

American craft beers usually have a fuller, more complex flavor than typical light American lagers because of the higher percentage of specialty malt and hop ingredients. Depending on how the brewmaster handles the hops, the beer's aroma may smell like citrus, flowers, or herbs. Specialty toasted and roasted malted barley contributes odors of caramel, biscuits, cocoa, coffee, honey, or even fresh-baked cookies. Specialty yeasts contribute aromatic and flavor characters such as clove, spice, banana, strawberry, and apples.

Brewmasters try to avoid skunky smells caused by a photochemical reaction, which means the beer has been exposed to light for too long. A winelike or wet cardboard smell or taste indicates old, stale beer; this stagnation speeds up if the beer is stored at warm temperatures. In a bar, if your draft beer has a sour, bacterial, or moldy flavor,

Marc Worona, brewmaster

Marc Worona first started whipping up his own brews back in his late teens, while he was studying microbiology at college. "That's one way of getting into it," he laughs. Little did he know one day he'd be doing just that for a living.

Once he graduated, he heard that Stoudt's Brewing Company in Adamstown, Pennsylvania, was looking for someone to work in quality control in their brewery lab. "I started working there, and basically moved up," he recalls. Later, Worona attended the Siebel Institute, a brewer school in Chicago.

What Worona likes best about being a brewmaster is the constant challenges and the opportunity for creativity. "I like the number of challenges," he says, "and it's very physical. You get a good workout, you get to be creative and do scientific things. Plus there are all kinds of maintenance issues that need to be addressed."

Even better, no workday is exactly the same as the next. "Between equipment breakdowns and the yeast—they're living organisms, they change from day to day and you have to manage them—being a brewmaster is full of challenges. It's exciting and very gratifying."

As a brewmaster, Worona is responsible for coming up with new recipes for different types of craft beers. "There were several in place when I first started," he notes, "but to keep current, to keep the beer tasting the same, you have to adjust the recipe." Brewmasters deal with various crops, different water chemistry, and different ingredients. "When it comes to new styles, we've done a lot of stuff over the last 10 years, not to mention tweaking the recipes we already had."

The best-selling beer at Stoudt's is the American Pale Ale, but Worona's favorite is the German-style wheat beer. "Year-round I enjoy the pilsner, but the pale ale is a close third," he says.

The only thing he doesn't like about his job is the irregular hours. "You're kind of like a doctor, you're always on call. If there's a problem, you can't leave until it's solved. And millions and trillions of little lives [the yeast] are hanging in the balance. Once you go home, everything is still plugging away here. If the lights flicker, I have to run in to make sure the pumps are still running. It never ends."

it's probably been poured from dirty tap hoses.

Typically, craft beer brewmasters think the big beer producers produce a bland pasteurized beverage that's designed to please the broadest possible taste. For economical reasons, they may substitute corn or rice for malted barley. Some big brewers actually speed up the fermentation process using enzymes to concentrate the beer, which is then watered down.

More than 1,400 craft breweries produce primarily all-malt beers. This includes brewpubs (brewery/restaurants), microbreweries (which produce less than 15,000 barrels per year), and specialty brewers. Even though craft beer accounts for only 3.2 percent of the beer marketplace versus more than an 11 percent share for imports, craft beer sales in 2004 increased by 6.34 million cases—1.78 million more new cases compared to imports.

The beer industry, which includes brewers, wholesalers, and retailers, is a major player in the U.S. economy—and the United States ranks number one in world beer production. More than 90 million Americans of legal drinking age enjoy beer.

Pitfalls

Being a brewmaster is a bit like being a medical intern—you're always on call, and you're the one in trouble if something goes wrong. If there is a problem, you can't go home until it's fixed.

Perks

If you love beer and science, being a brewmaster could be the perfect career for you. There's lots of creativity and room for developing your own recipes at a small craft brewery. If you choose to work at a large commercial brewery, you'll make good money for your efforts.

Get a Jump on the Job

If you think you might like to tinker with unique recipes at a craft brewery, you can start preparing by paying lots of attention during biology, microbiology, and chemistry class. Think about getting a summer job at a local craft brewery, working with kegs or even just sweeping up—anything to get a foot in the door. Read as much as you can about brewing beer, and choose a college where you can major in food science, microbiology, or fermentation science.

BUTCHER

OVERVIEW

When you go to your local grocery store, you probably don't give much thought to the person behind the meat counter as you look at the packages of shrink-wrapped steaks and chops lined up in the cooler. But they're vital to the process of turning large pieces of meat into specific items, such as steaks or roasts. You'll find butchers (also known as meat cutters) working in meat processing plants, grocery stores, or specialty meat shops.

The type of butchering you'll do depends on several factors. If you work in a meat-processing plant, for instance, you'll cut animal carcasses into large cuts sold to meat wholesalers. That type of work is normally done on assembly lines. Some industrial butchers also work in slaughterhouses, using stun guns and knives to kill cattle, sheep, goats, and hogs.

Butchers working at the wholesale level typically process large cuts of meat into smaller ones, which are then shipped to retail markets and grocery stores. Alternately, grocery stores can buy meat wholesale and have in-store butchers process it further. The trend these days, however, is for more processing to be done in the meatpacking plant or at the wholesale level, cutting down on the need for in-store butchers.

Butchers also grind meat to make hamburger and sausage, trim meat, remove bones from meat, and shape and tie roasts. Retail butchers may be responsible for arranging cut meat in cases, packaging cuts of meat, waiting on customers, and weighing and wrapping meat.

Knowledge of the nutritional values of different meats is useful, as butchers may have to answer such questions from

Brook Ridley, butcher

Brook Ridley has a bachelor of science degree in accounting, but there was never any question that he'd go into his family's meat business. "Basically, as part of a family business, there was no question of my learning the trade," Ridley says. "I had to learn to contribute to the business and to the family."

Ridley's family has been in the meat business for nearly 90 years, 50 of which included operating a meatpacking plant. Although they no longer have the packing plant, family members continue to train employees in the craft of butchering in their meat market, having turned out thousands of butchers over the years. Ridley uses his accounting skills in overseeing the business side of the market.

His market buys wholesale cuts of beef from large meat packers. Very particular about the quality of meat he buys, Ridley counts on a former employee who now works in a packing company warehouse to select choice animals for Ridley to purchase. Once the wholesale cuts arrive at Ridley's Butcher Shop, Ridley and other skilled butchers go about filling special orders and cutting meat to fill the case for walk-in customers. They pay close attention to different varieties, and how much wholesale meat they order, so that they are always prepared for business.

Ridley may spend some time consulting with a customer about the best meat to serve at an upcoming dinner or party. He often recommends cooking methods for various cuts of meat, and even passes along recipes that have been developed over the years by family members.

"Butchering is a trade that goes from the very first step to the delivered, finished product that a customer has ordered," Ridley says. "It is very rewarding to start with a side of beef and finish up with a rib eye steak, delivered to a single customer."

When the family business began back in 1920, meat was delivered to customers on a horse-drawn wagon. Today meat can be purchased in the meat market or ordered online. Meat is quick-frozen to assure maximum freshness; sealed and packed in sturdy, cooled, and insulated containers; and shipped out via express delivery.

While Ridley enjoys running the meat market as a long line of family members have done before him, jobs for meat cutters on a local level are in decline—a trend he sees occurring countrywide. "The profession of butcher is a dying trade," Ridley says. "There is a trend among the large retailers, basically started by Wal-Mart, to get their meat in already cut and packaged. Therefore, there is less and less of a need for local meat cutters because many people buy their meats from large, chain-type stores."

Still, other customers value the service and specialty cuts of meat they can find at a local meat market, assuring that some jobs for butchers will remain. "I still believe that there is a need for a local meat market that can provide a better grade of beef and better personal service," Ridley says. "I would recommend butchering as a career if a person wants to run his or her own business. Being a butcher for someone else typically demands long hours and hard work, but, as the owner, it is a good, honest trade that is quite rewarding."

Ridley suggests that a young person interested in owning a meat shop begin by learning the butchering trade, either through schooling or hands-on experience, and then get some business know-how. "The harder a person works, the better he or she can be, and the more product they can deliver," Ridley says. "It's very similar to life in general."

customers. In addition, it's helpful to know the cooking methods that work best for different cuts of meat. Some butcher shops deliver meat to customers, although most have drivers to do that, leaving the butcher free to work in the store.

Butchering is an old and traditional job, begun by necessity in the earliest periods of civilization. While butchering was traditionally done outdoors, in the United States it has moved inside for reasons of sanitation and convenience. Butchers and meat cutters must use extreme caution in their work because they use a variety of potentially dangerous equipment, including sharp knives, cleavers, meat saws, power cutters and slicers, and band saws. Many a butcher has suffered an injury in a moment of carelessness.

Pitfalls

Some people are put off by the notion of handling large cuts of raw meat, and many more by the prospect of actually killing the animal to be butchered. Butchering, however, has long been a respected profession. Do keep in mind, though, that the number of butchering jobs is expected to decline in the coming years. The working hours of butchers vary, but it may be necessary to work some evenings and weekends, especially if you work in retail.

Perks

Butchering is a service job that often allows face-to-face contact with customers, allowing you to interact with and help people on a regular basis. Cutting meat allows you to engage in hands-on work. Unless you're on a meat-cutting assembly line, the work tends to be varied and fairly social.

Get a Jump on the Job

Study meat charts so you can learn the different parts of the animals from which particular cuts of meat are taken. When you're old enough, get a job in a grocery store and ask to work in the meat department, or apply at a meat market and let the butcher know that you're interested in learning the job.

BUTTERBALL TURKEY TALK-LINE EXPERT

OVERVIEW

If you've ever helped out your mom or dad in the kitchen with a half-frozen turkey on Thanksgiving and wondered how on earth it was going to be defrosted in time for dinner—the Butterball Turkey Talk-Line experts are there to help!

Staffed with nearly 50 seasoned home economists, nutritionists, and turkey experts during November and December, the Butterball Turkey Talk-Line is available for first-time cooks and seasoned pros alike and provides answers to all turkey-related questions. The experts range in age from 20 through retirement; two-thirds are either registered dieticians or home economics teachers, and 43 percent have a master's degree in a related field. If you love to cook and have a yen to chat about it, this job could be for you!

Back when the talk-line started 25 years ago, 800 numbers were still quite unusual. The Butterball people realized lots of consumers had questions about cooking turkeys, so they decided to try an 800 number, thinking maybe people would feel comfortable calling it. Butterball hired six home economists that year, parked them at regular desks with rolodexes of information, and ended up fielding 11,000 calls from frenzied turkey preparers that year! Today, turkey experts respond to more than 100,000 questions during the

holiday season from November through December. These days, Butterball's talk-line experts also staff computers, answering e-mailed questions within 24 hours during the holiday crunch time (November 22 to 25 and December 22 to 25), or within 48 hours during the rest of the Butterball Turkey Talk-Line season.

Cooking is all about the latest fad, so you shouldn't be surprised to hear that each year, experts have to keep up with the various turkey trends—such as the turducken that was all the rage in 2004.

AT A GLANCE

Salary Range
Unspecified.

Education/Experience
At least a bachelor's degree, preferably in nutrition or home economics. A master's degree and cooking experience are also helpful.

Personal Attributes
Warm, engaging speaking voice and personality; should be an excellent communicator and enjoy talking on the phone; interest in cooking, food, and food safety.

Requirements
Expert knowledge of how to cook turkey. Experience in home economics or nutrition is required. You must live within commuting distance of Chicago, where the talk-line center is located.

Outlook
There aren't a huge number of jobs for this two-month holiday season stint—Butterball typically uses 50 talk-line experts, but the popularity of the talk-line (several hundred thousand calls per holiday period) ensures it will likely be in place for the foreseeable future.

Mary Clingman, director of the Butterball Turkey Talk-Line

Mary Clingman was a home-ec major with a warm, engaging personality who loved to share with others on the phone—so joining up with the Butterball Turkey Talk-Line was a natural for her. After moving back to Illinois, she decided she really wanted to start doing something with her major, and when she heard about the talk-line, realized it was the perfect two-month opportunity for her.

The turkey talk-line year starts in October, when all the talk-line ladies head to Chicago for a few days of Butterball University. "That's a fun thing if you like to cook," Clingman says. Experts who have already attended previous years may be asked to cook a turkey in a way they've never done before, or take a magazine recipe and try it out. "We do get calls from people who are turning turkeys over, covering or not covering them—these may be perfectly safe methods, but what is it like?" Clingman says. "At Butterball U, one of the talk-line ladies will try out each of the methods to see."

At the yearly training, the women line up and cook 10 different turkeys 10 different ways, testing recipes and seeing what works and what doesn't. "People want Thanksgiving to be special, so they want to do a wonderful new recipe. If it's not written totally correctly, it won't work out. It's good for us to experience that during practice." There's also a real pleasure in getting back together with the talk-line ladies, most of whom haven't seen each other since last year's talk-line. "Getting together in October, it's like old home week," Clingman says. "Lot of times I haven't seen most of these gals until then, and I do miss them."

When the talk-line opens in early November, the first calls are typically from organized women wondering how much turkey to buy for their guests. Then there are the unexpected calls. "I got a call from a gentleman from the south who wanted to know if he could cook a turkey that he'd had frozen in 1969!" (Clingman told him no, although turkeys frozen for a year are still perfectly edible.)

The talk-line ladies keep track of who's asking what. "The number one question people have is about thawing," Clingman reports, "but the number two question is about food safety, which I think is great. Of course, it's not like they're calling up saying: 'Tell me about food safety.' Instead, they say: 'Here's what I did—just how sick will I get?'" Clingman's favorite calls are on Thanksgiving Day. "The calls can become pretty complicated," she says. "We might be on a call for half an hour, 45 minutes. Sometimes if someone has done one thing wrong, they maybe did other things wrong, too. By the time we work through all that, quite a lot of time may pass. But we'll try to find the answer, because the last thing we want to say is 'throw it out!'"

Sometimes, there's just no alternative, however, if the turkey hasn't been handled safely. "The thing to remember is that turkey is a perishable item," she says. "You want to have it either very cold or very hot." It's in that "just-warm" middle of the road area that trouble can begin. Clingman recalls a woman in Georgia who had to prepare a turkey for tailgate parties two weekends in a row. "The first weekend, everyone got sick," Clingman says. Why? She took the turkey out of the oven, wrapped it in foil, and placed it in the refrigerator. The next day when she

(continues)

(continued)

took it out, the turkey still had not properly chilled—meaning it spent all night in that dangerous "just-warm" area where bacteria can breed.

"The talk-line is a great group of ladies," she says. "You have to be somebody who likes to talk to people. It amazes me—they'll be talking on the phone for the whole eight hours, yet when they take a break, they're in the break room talking to a group of ladies about recipes."

Then there's the basting issue. "We talk about the fact that you don't really have to baste a turkey," Clingman says. "Turkey skin is like a raincoat. Whatever you put on the skin doesn't really get into the meat much—it slides off into the drippings. I've talked to people who baste every 15 minutes! So I had one of the gals basting every 15 minutes to see if it improved the flavor." (It didn't.) "Sometimes, we get callers from charities who might be making 10 turkeys for different families in their town. They'll want to know how to get meals out to people in a safe way. To be able to call us and get some guidance is really such a big help."

Fads may come and go, but turkey is always popular, year after year. "It's delicious and economical, and good for you—high protein and low fat," Clingman says. "It's also unique. Cooking a turkey kind of makes the meal an event, and the house smells so good while it's in the oven," Clingman says. "More than 91 percent of Americans eat turkey for Thanksgiving. People take this day very seriously. It's a very important time." The company, with its eye on newest trends, now also gets lots of hits on its Web site; experts answer about 10,000 e-mails throughout the year. Regular staffers go in and work on the talk-line, but each also take turns answering e-mail questions from home. But the talk-line still pulls in the calls. "It's a very, very popular thing," Clingman says. "People have learned over years to trust 1-800-BUTTERBALL.

"The crescendo builds each day, and culminates on Thanksgiving. That day we'll talk to 10,000 people. It starts at 6 a.m. with people on the East Coast, and we quit at 6 p.m. with people from the West Coast. During that day, there will be callers in the middle of snow storms, power outages, babies being delivered, people who thought they were having four guests and find out it's really 24. We get to share Thanksgiving with a lot of nice people. Then we go home and our husbands are doing the cooking. They feel sorry for us, but the turkey is cooked and the house is picked up!"

This difficult-to-prepare Cajun specialty calls for a deboned chicken to be stuffed inside a deboned duck to be stuffed inside a deboned turkey, with different dressings in between each layer. This is one example of why it's vital that each year the turkey talk-line experts bone up on the latest turkey cooking fads by cooking turkeys themselves. In October, everyone attends "Butterball University" for a few days of intense information sessions and actual hands-on turkey preparations. This cooking experience means that if you've heard of a brand-new way to cook a turkey—well, one of the turkey experts at Butterball has probably already cooked up a turkey following that method, and he or she will be able to help you out.

Becoming a Butterball Turkey Talk-Line expert is fairly straightforward if you're already a home economist, teacher, or a registered dietician. Spanish-speaking experts are also in demand. Typically, you'll be asked to sign on for a two-month-a-year stint (November and December, prime turkey-eating months) at the call center located outside Chicago.

Calls often center around some improper cooking methods or odd new ways of cooking turkey that just aren't safe. For example, one recent "bad idea" involves popping the turkey in a 450-degree oven for an hour, and then turning the oven down to 200 and cooking it overnight. It's a bad idea because—for safety reasons—a turkey needs to be fully cooked within four hours.

Some of the most common questions the turkey experts field include:

"I'm having 24 guests—how much turkey should I buy?" (Answer: Visit the Butterball.com Web site, which boasts a helpful calculator—you type in the number of people, they'll calculate your turkey and stuffing needs.)

"Fresh or frozen?" (Answer: Depends on whether you care about thawing hassles with the frozen bird; fresh Butterballs are also all natural.)

"What's the best way to thaw a turkey?" (Answer: In the fridge, one day per four pounds.)

Occasionally—rarely—one of the talk-line experts doesn't know the answer. When that happens, he or she will put the caller on hold and ask the others in the room for help.

Pitfalls

You'll be busy and talking for almost your entire shift during peak call-in periods, and you'll likely have to work Thanksgiving Day and Christmas Day—so you'll need a friend or family member willing to pop your own turkey in the oven.

Perks

If you love to cook and you enjoy educating others—no matter how frenzied—this can be a really fun job to have for two months out of the year. The talk-line staffers become good friends who enjoy sharing recipes, cooking ideas, and friendship.

Get a Jump on the Job

Spend as much time in the kitchen as you can, learning how to cook. Take home ec classes if your high school offers it. Get as much experience around food and cooking as possible: work in a restaurant, help your mom or dad at home, and bone up on food safety issues by reading articles and books on the topic.

CAKE DECORATOR

OVERVIEW

If you've ever seen a really beautiful cake at a special birthday party, wedding, or other celebration, chances are it was the work of a professional cake decorator. Cake decorators are self-employed, work for grocery stores and independent bakeries, and in restaurants and hotels. A cake decorator may have one or two jobs a week, or many, depending on circumstances.

Cake decorators are expected to be able to mix the icings and frostings they'll use to on their cakes. Once the icing or frosting is made, it must be carefully and evenly applied to the cake. Then the cake is ready to be decorated, using specially tinted frostings and specialty equipment such as piping bags, cutters, brushes, and nozzles. Some cake decorators use fresh flowers and other items in addition to icing.

Many cake decorators also make their own cakes, although in some restaurants and hotels it might be that a pastry chef does the baking and the decorator is only responsible for decorating.

Decorating cakes is fun, but it's not all sugar and spice. There's a certain amount of pressure involved with cake decorating, because the cake most likely is very important to the person who ordered it. When a customer orders a specially made and decorated cake, he or she generally expects it to be of high quality, look and taste great, and accurately reflect

AT A GLANCE

Salary Range

The average salary for a cake decorator is about $21,000, with the highest 10 percent earning more than $33,500, and the lowest 10 percent earning less than $14,000. Salary depends on how well known you are, the area in which you work, and other factors.

Education/Experience

While there are no specific educational requirements for cake decorators, training at a culinary school or other school offering culinary arts is recommended. Many culinary schools have baking programs, which include decorating. Some community colleges and city colleges also offer culinary programs specializing in baking and decorating. Cake decorators sometimes work as apprentices and learn on the job.

Personal Attributes

Because most cake decorators also make the cakes they decorate, you should enjoy both practical and creative work. You should also be well organized and somewhat business-minded. You'll need to be able to keep track of orders, arrange for pickups and deliveries, order necessary supplies, bill for your services, and so forth.

Requirements

Some cake decorators work from their homes, which may require state licensing. People who work in food service may be required to undergo a physical to make sure they have no diseases that could be spread to the public.

Outlook

The number of jobs for cake decorators is expected to increase at about an average rate through 2012, according to government statistics.

the celebration. Accuracy is especially important. When a cake shows up at a party decorated with the wrong message,

Anne Louise Reinert, cake decorator

Anne Louise Reinert has been working in some aspect of the restaurant industry since she was 15 years old, and she's been baking and decorating celebration cakes for 18 years. During that time, she's created thousands of cakes for birthday parties, weddings, anniversary celebrations, graduation parties, first communion celebrations, Bar and Bat Mitzvahs, holiday parties, and other special occasions.

She enjoys her work, she says, because it's always different, and each job brings its own challenges and opportunities. "I really like the sense of creativity and accomplishment, and I know I can keep getting better at what I do," Reinert says. "I never want to get to the point where I do every cake the same way and am no longer working at getting better and better at my work."

Working with a small staff from her bakery in West Reading, Pennsylvania, Reinert bakes, designs, and decorates all the cakes she sells. Her average cake takes about 10 hours all together, including the mixing, baking, cooling, and decorating. While she is busy year-round, holidays and the wedding season (the summer months) keep her pretty much tied to her shop. "You have to be willing to work long days and a lot of weekends, that's for sure," Reinert says.

Because weddings typically are held on Fridays, Saturdays, and Sundays, her workweek intensifies starting on Wednesday during wedding season. "I start preparing my butter creams [icing] on Wednesday, and we bake the cakes the day of the wedding, unless it's a very early one. You have to leave time for the cakes to cool before they can be decorated."

On a recently made wedding cake, Reinert swirled the icing to create a wave effect, and decorated the cake with white chocolate, molded into seashell shape.

"It's fun," she says. "I'll try to create whatever look the customer wants. There are all sorts of things you can do."

Reinert was trained at the Culinary Institute of America in Hyde Park, New York, and earned certification as a chef with a specialization in pastry. However, this training is somewhat unusual for a cake decorator. "It's unusual that someone who is a chef also bakes," she explains. "Most chefs don't bake, and most pastry chefs don't decorate their own cakes."

Reinert has continued her culinary training over the years, working to be licensed as a Kosher chef, and learning about different types of food allergies and how to deal with them. "I have kind of a unique niche," she says.

While culinary training is important and useful, Reinert advises developing a strong art background if you're interested in cake decorating, and recommends studying graphic design and tuning into colors. Having some knowledge of fresh flowers, such as which hold up best, which are nontoxic, and which are readily available, is also useful.

Mainly, Reinert says, a cake decorator has to be willing to work hard, be able to communicate effectively with clients, and be available when necessary. "I spend a lot of time on my feet and a lot of time answering to clients," Reinert says.

While decorating cakes requires time, energy, and effort, Reinert says she can't imagine doing any other work. Baking and decorating cakes for special occasions is happy work, she explains, and she enjoys sharing celebratory occasions with her customers. "It takes a lot of hard work, practice, and perseverance, but I can't think of anything better," Reinert says. "It's a good way to earn a living."

that customer may take their business elsewhere in the future.

Cake decorators who are well known and in demand often work long hours, especially in busy wedding and holiday seasons. Still, if you enjoy baking and decorating cakes, this job can offer flexibility and financial rewards. It is possible to decorate cakes at home, which is how freelance decorators work; some small bakeries also may allow you to set your own schedule.

Pitfalls

There can be a lot of pressure during busy times, and customers can be demanding, especially if the cake is for an important event, such as a wedding. If you work for yourself, you'll have some start-up costs, and you'll need to keep up with the administrative tasks associated with running a business.

Perks

Cake decorators tend to be artistic and creative people who love showcasing their talents for appreciative customers. Once you've become known and established as a premier cake decorator, you'll be able to be a little pickier about which jobs you take, perhaps making your schedule a little less demanding.

Get a Jump on the Job

There's nothing like hands-on experience. Volunteer to make and decorate cakes for family birthdays and other celebrations. Read some books about decorating cakes and apply what you learn. When you're old enough, apply for a job in the bakery of your local supermarket or with an independent bakery. Express your interest in decorating cakes, and watch as the experienced decorators work.

CHEESE MAKER

OVERVIEW

As far back as 6,000 B.C., ancient humans were making cheese. The delicious dairy product was probably discovered accidentally by nomadic tribes carrying milk in bags made from animal skins on their travels. In the hot sun, the milk would curdle, and the constant movement of the bags would break up the curd. Eventually, the milk would have separated into a watery liquid (whey) and a solid sort of cheese (curds).

Archeologists have found murals in Egyptian tombs from about 2,000 B.C. depicting cheese and butter being made. Of course, cheese and cheese-making methods have changed dramatically in the past 8,000 years.

While the basic theory of cheese making hasn't changed, cheese makers now use sophisticated machinery and modern technology to produce all sorts of cheeses. Large operations use advanced process control and recording systems to monitor cheese production, often operating equipment from a control room. Small cheese-making operations are much more hands-on, requiring skill and knowledge about the process of making cheese.

Basically, cheese is simply processed milk—but the process of turning milk into cheese requires the close supervision and attention of a trained cheese maker. While the very large cheese-making facilities are fully automated, many small cheese-making operations still use the traditional methods of changing milk into cheese.

AT A GLANCE

Salary Range

The salary for a cheese maker varies widely, depending on the setting in which the person works and the level of his or her training and experience. A beginning cheese maker can expect to earn about $25,000 a year, while an experienced cheese maker can make about $60,000. Master cheese makers who work for large cheese manufacturing companies or have established, widespread reputations can expect to earn even more.

Education/Experience

A degree in food science or food technology might give you an advantage, as will skills in engineering, microbiology, or chemistry. Normally, however, you'll just need to get trained as a cheese maker, either privately or through courses run by a state-related organization such as a cooperative extension service.

Personal Attributes

Making cheese requires skill, patience, and hard physical work. You'll need to be in good condition and be able to work long hours when necessary. It will also be helpful if you're inquisitive and eager to continue learning new methods and techniques of your craft.

Requirements

Some states require cheese makers to be licensed, requiring official training and apprenticeship.

Outlook

Jobs in all areas of food production are expected to increase by about 5 percent through 2012. Artisan cheese makers (that is, small, specialty producers) will probably see a more rapid growth.

Normally, the process begins when milk is either delivered to a cheese-making operation or is obtained on site. Most of the cheese we eat in this country is made

Robert Wills, cheese maker

Robert Wills—known as Bob to most people—has been a licensed cheese maker for about 15 years, and is president of Cedar Grove Cheese, Inc. Wills received the Master Cheese Maker designation about five years ago, after completing extensive course work and other requirements.

Cedar Grove, which started out as a small, family-owned cheese-making operation, has grown to be a small factory employing nine full-time cheese makers. Still, Wills says, they use primarily traditional, artisan methods of cheese-making to turn out about 15,000 pounds of cheese each day.

At Cedar Grove, milk is delivered at night, and it's then that the cheese making begins. The company makes their cheese in the cool of the night because the factory isn't air-conditioned. (Contaminants could enter the factory through air conditioning vents.) And by working through the night, the cheese can be ready by late afternoon, when Cedar Grove hires high school students to help package it and clean up the factory. In addition, Cedar Grove is known for its fresh curds, which can be made in about six hours. Working overnight means the curds are finished by early morning, when they can be packaged and distributed to stores at their very freshest. "I'm not sure that every factory works that way," Wills says, "but working at night seems to us to be the way to do it."

Although Wills loves making cheese, he warns that the work is physically difficult and requires patience and fortitude. And you have to be willing to stay on top of all the newest regulations, such as food safety. "Dealing with government regulations covering milk pricing and food safety is very challenging and sometimes frustrating," Wills says. "And it's a lot of physical labor, long hours, and small profit margins."

Wills recommends that someone interested in learning to make cheese get on-the-job training from a licensed cheese maker, along with training in engineering, microbiology, and chemistry. Perhaps most important, Wills says, is to have a passion for making cheese and a sense of creativity.

"Cheese making is a lot like winemaking," Wills says. "There is a great similarity between these professions, in that they are both combinations of art and science."

A renewed interest in small-scale, artisan cheese making is providing new opportunities for those willing to devote much time and effort to learning and mastering the craft. "There is a lot of room for developing unique products and being very creative," Wills says. "Here in Wisconsin, we take great pride in our cheese heritage and in our dedication to the art of cheese making."

from cow's milk, but the milk of sheep and goats can also be used. The milk is usually filtered and pasteurized to kill any potentially harmful bacteria, and then pumped into tanks. Once the tanks are filled, a culture is added to the milk that causes it to sour. In the souring process, the milk sugars (lactose) turns into lactic acid. The amount of lactic acid in the milk helps to determine what type of cheese will be made, so it's important for the cheese maker to monitor it carefully.

Lactic acid is also important to cheese making because it activates rennet, an enzyme that causes milk to coagulate. Once rennet is added to the milk, it doesn't take long for the milk to thicken to about the consistency of pudding. Again, a cheese maker keeps a close watch on the process to make sure it's proceeding as desired. Once the milk has thickened to the desired consistency, wire knives within the tanks are pulled back and forth, breaking the thickened milk into very small pieces. The tiny pieces are called *curds*.

The curds are cooked until they separate from the watery material, called whey, and the whey is drained out of the tanks. Once the whey has been removed, the cheese maker adds salt, which slows down the process of the lactic acid and adds flavor to the cheese. (If salt weren't added, the acid would eventually cause the cheese to crumble.) The curds are then pressed and processed, after which the cheese maker puts them into metal forms called hoops. While in the hoops, pressure forces the curds together to form cheese, which can then be cut into blocks, stored, and sold.

All cheese making follows these basic steps, but each cheese maker develops his or her own personal methods and tricks. You can add a variety of flavorings to cheese, store it in ways that vary its taste and texture, and do many other things to create your own trademark cheese. Cheese making is much like winemaking in that it combines art and science, and you can continue learning and refining your skills for many, many years.

The duties and responsibilities of cheese makers vary tremendously, depending on the size and scope of the operation. In a small cheese-making facility, the cheese maker might be responsible for everything from milking cows to sealing and storing the finished product. You might also find yourself keeping track of the business side of the operation, such as ordering supplies, keeping track of customers and orders, and so forth. In a very large operation, you may have only one particular duty in the cheese-making operation.

Regardless of whether you'd be working for a large manufacturer or a small artisan cheese-making operation, hygiene is extremely important when producing cheese. Contaminants could easily enter the milk, curds, or cheese, creating the potential for serious illness.

Pitfalls

It can take quite a while to become an accomplished cheese maker, which means you may not make much money until you've become known and have gained considerable experience. Many cheese makers maintain other jobs until they become established in the industry.

Perks

If you work for a small cheese-making operation, your responsibilities are likely to be varied, meaning that your days will be interesting. And once you've built a reputation as a cheese maker, you should have no trouble finding jobs.

Get a Jump on the Job

If you're traveling near a cheese-making area such as Wisconsin or parts of New York or Vermont (or you're lucky enough to live there), visit a facility to see firsthand what a cheese maker does. Some operations give tours that allow you to see exactly how cheese is made. You can also read about cheese making. (See the "Cheese Maker" section of "Read All About It" at the back of this book.)

CHEF-INNKEEPER

OVERVIEW

You'd be amazed at how many people dream of owning and operating their own bed-and-breakfast or inn. Have you ever thought: "I'd love to open a bed-and-breakfast! It will be fun to entertain guests in my home, and since I cook and clean anyway, what could be so hard?" Well, lots of others before you have thought the same thing.

What's important to consider, of course, is that there's also a business side of innkeeping. An inn or B and B may seem relaxing, but it also involves mounds of paperwork, constant interruptions during the day, and piles of laundry waiting to be finished. There are taxes and regulations to juggle, fresh food to buy, cook, serve, and recipes and menus to plan.

It's also a very personal sort of career—you'll be sharing your home with guests, and you'll be very involved with them.

The basic routine of a chef-innkeeper is pretty similar across the country: You rise with the roosters (around 5 a.m.) so you can start cooking and serving breakfasts that you've created, trying to make the recipes as innovative and tasty as you can. Then it's on to cleaning the rooms and doing the laundry (assuming you don't have a staff to do this), shopping for food for the next meal, and recipe and meal planning. Don't forget banking, bookkeeping, advertising, and marketing, while handling check-ins, reservations, and other management issues. You may think it's great not to

AT A GLANCE

Salary Range

Income varies wildly, depending on the size and success of the B and B or inn, its location, and so on. A chef-innkeeper who owns his or her own place may expect to earn between $40,000 and $70,000-plus a year, although highly successful and experienced innkeeper chefs could earn much more.

Education/Experience

Educational requirements for chefs should include completion of a culinary arts program at a recognized culinary schools, or a degree in food service and hotel management from a university. Today, most chefs agree that a certificate or diploma from either a four-year college in a culinary, food service, or nutritional-related field, or completion of a culinary arts program, is almost mandatory.

Personal Attributes

Being your own boss as a chef and an innkeeper isn't as stressful as the job of a restaurant chef, but there's still pressure. You should have a strong interest in food, enjoy cooking, and also love people and have an interest in innkeeping. You must have patience to try recipes over and over until they are perfect, and the ability to interact with other people. As with many jobs, a good sense of humor and a gregarious personality is useful.

Requirements

Good business skills, cooking ability, and interest in people.

Outlook

Good. There are always opportunities in the ever-changing world of inns and B and Bs, provided you have the money and time to invest.

Carl Kosko, chef and bed-and-breakfast owner

Nestled in Lancaster County, Pennsylvania, in the heart of the little village of New Holland (deep in Amish country), you'll find the Harvest Moon Bed and Breakfast, where European hospitality joins forces with American ingenuity, run by chefs Carl Kosko and his wife Marlies.

Carl grew up in Maryland and attended the Rhode Island School of Design (RISD) cooking school. Upon graduation he was hired by the New England Inn, becoming the youngest head chef in the restaurant's history. Within a few years he turned the restaurant into an award-winning hot spot. It was at the inn that he met his future wife Marlies, a native of Germany. Marlies had been the fourth generation of the Hornsteiner family to own the Gasthof Mulhauser, an inn located beside the ski slopes of Bavaria. Marlies studied cooking and hotel management before traveling to the United States to work at the New England Inn.

Together, the two of them decided to combine their love of cooking and of running an inn by opening their own B&B.

"I like being a chef and working at an inn," he says. "I always loved inns, and the two together—cooking and owning an inn—you get the best of both worlds. You have the time to be creative and make some wonderful things, but you have the time to get out and talk to the guests, too."

While most people can find something they don't like about their job, Carl simply loves what he does. "I own my own business, so if I didn't like it I'd be in trouble," he laughs. "Obviously, there are days better than others."

While he recommends the career as chef-innkeeper to anyone, he cautions that it does entail quite a bit of work. "Don't go into it thinking: 'Wouldn't it be nice just to run a B and B and be a chef?' You have to be able to be with people," he says. It's important to really love the job because you'll be spending quite a bit of your time doing it, he notes. "Just yesterday, I was up with a leaky pipe until about 11 p.m., and I'd been up since 6 a.m. Then I had to get up this morning to cook breakfast at 6 a.m. again."

Although lots of people think running a B and B sounds like a fun, romantic way to spend your life, Carl cautions that you need a solid education and experience before opening your doors. "Especially in today's world, you really need to have specific training. Back when I went, 20 years ago, you could get into the trade by studying at a restaurant and learning under other chefs. Nowadays you have to go to culinary school. People want to see the certificates and degrees.

"But if this is your dream, and you really want it, it's a wonderful career."

have to worry about being tied down to the corporate 9-to-5 job, until you realize you've traded those hours for a seven-day-a-week commitment with 12-to-18 hour workdays and an office you can't escape.

Pitfalls

The hours can be killer—seven days a week, and you're on call 24 hours a day. Most chef-innkeepers live in their B and Bs, so you're inviting strangers into your home on a daily basis. And while serving the public can be fun, you'll also inevitably get cranky, demanding, difficult visitors.

Perks

If you love people and you love cooking, chef-innkeepers will tell you there's no better job on earth. You own your own business, and you'll have the time and incentive to get everything just right.

Get a Jump on the Job

Read everything you can about cooking, recipe development, and running an inn or bed-and-breakfast. When you're old enough, get a job in a restaurant and make it clear that you're interested in cooking. Cook at home and experiment with recipes or try to come up with your own recipes. Or try getting an after-school job at an inn, B and B, or hotel, to get an idea of what it's like to run this kind of establishment.

CHOCOLATIER

OVERVIEW

For thousands of years the world has been in love with chocolate, revered for its exquisite flavor and texture. Chocolate originated in Mexico and Central America, where the Mayans were eating chocolate as early as 500 A.D. When Cortez invaded Mexico, he noticed that Montezuma, the ruler of the Aztecs, was swallowing endless flagons of frothy *chocolatl* (chocolate) every day, made with either water or wine and seasoned with vanilla, pimiento, and chili pepper. Montezuma served *chocolatl* to his Spanish guests in gold goblets. This chocolate was fairly bitter to the Europeans' taste, but they soon learned how to add sugar to sweeten it up. Although this new beverage was typically far too expensive for any but the wealthiest to afford, by the late 17th century it was widely consumed among European nobility. In 1828 a Dutch chocolate maker patented a new way of creating powdered chocolate with a dark color and mild taste; a few decades later, the Swiss started making solid chocolate candy. In prerevolutionary New England, the first chocolate factory was established, and soon the United States was churning out more of the sweet stuff than anywhere else in the world.

Today, the world consumes some 3 million tons of cocoa beans each year, and the worldwide demand for chocolate continues to grow. Artisanal chocolatiers are popping up across America as the country's love affair with chocolate gets stronger. Just like boutique vintners, this new type of handmade chocolate producer

focuses on turning out limited quantities produced by hand with the best ingredients and a great deal of flair. The chocolates are decorated with delicate flowers and gold leaf and lovingly placed in fashionably designed gift boxes tied up with special paper and bows. These handmade, high-end chocolates, made from natural ingredients with no preservatives, are filled with intense flavors such as Earl Gray tea, balsamic vinegar, praline, or Zinfandel. Committed to working in small batches using traditional techniques to better control the quality of the product, the chocolatier hand-dips each piece in milk, dark, or white chocolate. These high-end

Jean-Marc Gorce, chocolatier

Jean-Marc Gorce spent his childhood stealing chocolate out of the kitchen drawer, never realizing he would one day make a living by creating fine chocolate creations in a pocket-sized truffle shop in San Francisco's North Beach—XOX Truffles. Named one of the top 10 chocolate-makers in the United States by *Chocolatier* magazine, Gorce owns the shop with his wife Casimira, where he offers 21 varieties of truffles. (A truffle is a small, hand-rolled chocolate with a dense ganache center.)

"My favorite thing about working with chocolate is the smell," he says. "When you walk in the shop and you smell the chocolate. If you're a chocoholic like I am, there's no such thing as too much chocolate. It's the perfect job for me."

Gorce began as former chef de cuisine at Fringale and at the Westin St. Francis. He and his wife opened their small shop in 1998; he makes the truffles while Casimira handles the marketing chores and serves customers. The chocolate he uses is processed in France from cocoa beans grown on the Ivory Coast. To make his truffles, he pours boiling cream over the chocolate and coffee, nuts, or liqueur, and then cools it and rolls it in cocoa powder, producing tiny bite-sized truffles. Gorce makes 27 flavors of truffles, including two with white chocolate and six made with soy milk—a nod to vegans, who avoid food made with milk or milk products.

Casimira's favorite is a truffle filled with white ganache infused with Madagascar vanilla and hand-dipped in creamy French white chocolate; Jean Marc's top choice is a cognac truffle. Recently named as one of the six best chocolate makers in the world, Jean-Marc is a friendly sort of chocolatier, waving to everyone who passes his shop. Women, in particular, seem to love his candy, and he loves the cosmopolitan atmosphere of North Beach. "It's really rewarding," he says, "and it makes it all worthwhile that people like my chocolate. It's always the positive attention, so I like that! It makes me feel good every day."

chocolates can cost from $30 to more than $60 a pound.

Typically, specialty chocolate makers are former chefs or Europeans who came to this country with a background in fine chocolate—but more and more candy makers are getting into the business from other fields. To be successful, you'll need to understand ingredients and how to produce a consistent gourmet chocolate each and every time. You also need to understand the chemistry of chocolate, what determines its flavor and texture, and how to handle it so that the final product

comes out looking shiny and without a disfiguring white bloom.

Of course, making the chocolate is only part of the battle. You also need to understand how to market your product and how to run your business. No matter how fabulous your chocolate, if nobody knows where to get them—or even that they exist—you'll be out of luck.

Whether producing chocolate commercially or artisanally, you typically go about it in the same way. To make cocoa, you remove some of the cocoa butter, but to produce dark, bittersweet, and milk

Frequently featured in local and national magazines and newspapers, Gorce was interviewed in February 2005 for a segment of *Roker on the Road* for the Food Network. "We get a lot of press coverage saying my chocolate is good," Gorce admits, "so as long as it's continuing, I'm happy!"

In fact, the only thing he doesn't like about the job is the occasional customer who doesn't understand fine chocolate, and balks at paying a premium price for his handmade creations. "Once in a while at the store, someone argues with me about paying $32 for a pound of chocolate, but those people don't know any better. I don't like dealing with people who don't know anything about dealing with good chocolate, and when they don't, they make silly comments."

If you're interested in working with chocolate, it's important to understand that it involves hard work, Gorce says. "It's not easy," he cautions "but it's all worth it in the end. Like anything else, nothing comes easy. But you can be independent, do something people really enjoy, and it's very rewarding. You make people feel good. It's better than being a dentist!"

Students interested in the world of chocolate and dreaming of opening their own chocolate shop would do well to take some business courses along with the cooking instruction, Gorce recommends. In his case, his wife handles the business end of the shop, and he knows how important good business and marketing ideas can be. "You can be very talented, but if you don't know how to sell your chocolate, you'll just stay in your little neighborhood and do nothing." In addition to business classes, an apprenticeship with a chocolatier or a good cooking school with classes on chocolate making is a good idea, he recommends.

Gorce is a man who truly loves his work. "We believe in the purity of back-to-basics and capturing the authenticity of a true French truffle," he explains "I love creating new chocolate flavors, I make them all, and making truffles is fun, selling it is fun. It's nice when people try it in front of you and say all kinds of nice things—I would recommend it to anyone."

chocolate, you add cocoa butter. Besides enhancing the flavor, this extra cocoa butter makes the chocolate more fluid. Along with the cocoa butter, you combine unsweetened chocolate, sugar, and vanilla, melting and combining the ingredients in a large mixing machine until the mass has the consistency of dough.

The most common type of chocolate is milk chocolate, which goes through essentially the same mixing process as other types of chocolate, except that less unsweetened chocolate is used and more milk is added.

Once the ingredients are added, the mixture then travels through a series of heavy rollers to refine it to a smooth paste ready for conching. Conching is a flavor development process in which the chocolate is kneaded; it gets its name from the shell-like shape of the containers. The machines used in this process (called *conches*) have heavy rollers that plow back and forth through the chocolate mass anywhere from a few hours to several days. Under regulated speeds, these rollers can produce different degrees of agitation and aeration in developing and modifying the chocolate flavors.

Some chocolatiers emulsify their product, either replacing conching or supplementing the process. The emulsifying machine works like an eggbeater to break up sugar crystals and other particles in the chocolate mixture to give it a fine, velvety smoothness.

After the emulsifying or conching machines, the mixture must be tempered—heated, cooled, and reheated—and then poured into molds of various shapes and sizes. Fillings for chocolate are poured in carefully and then covered with a coating of chocolate. The molded chocolate must then be cooled at a fixed rate to keep the flavor intact.

All chocolate manufacturers must follow government rules, which specify the minimum content of the chocolate liquor and milk, along with strict rules about flavorings and other ingredients. Chocolatiers may add hazelnuts, walnuts, almonds, pine kernels, pistachios, and fruits, such as raisins, oranges, cherries, pineapples, and lemons.

Many chocolates contain a liquid center surrounded by a sugar coating. To make these chocolates, the chocolatier spreads out wide sheets of starch powder, making small indentations and filling them with a solution of hot sugar syrup and liqueur or fruit juice. After one to two days, a complete coating of sugar has formed, completely enveloping the liqueur.

The starch powder is then removed and the centers are then covered with chocolate.

Chocolates with layer fillings have several separate flavors. The individual fillings are first spread out in broad layers on top of each other, and are then cut to the right shape and size. These chocolates are often sold in this form without any additional chocolate coating.

Pitfalls

If you want to set up your own chocolate shop, you'll need to have a head for business as well as being creative and a good chef.

Perks

Hand-creating delicate chocolates can be an enormously fulfilling, creative job if you love chocolate and you love to cook.

Get a Jump on the Job

There's nothing to stop you from buying some premium chocolate bars and a few recipe books, and practicing with your own concoctions in your home kitchen. The more experience you have with chocolate, the better. You can try getting a job in a local chocolatier's shop and learning as much as you can from the chef, and then go on to major in food science or hotel/restaurant management in college. Alternatively, you can learn a lot about chocolate at a culinary institute.

CIDER MAKER

OVERVIEW

Apple cider production operations range from small, hand-operated presses that make a couple of gallons of cider at a time to very large, completely automated systems that turn out thousands of gallons. Most operations fall somewhere in the middle of those extremes.

Some cider makers, especially large, commercial ones, buy their apples from orchards. Other cider makers grow their own apples. Some cider makers are primarily orchard operators who press cider as a way to use up extra apples, or those they may not be able to sell because they are blemished or otherwise deficient.

In North America, sweet cider is the juice that is freshly pressed from apples. It is an amber-golden color, not fermented, and contains no alcohol. Most commercial cider is pasteurized or treated with ultraviolet light to kill any potentially harmful bacteria. It cannot, however, be diluted with water or another liquid, or it's no longer considered apple cider.

Fermented cider becomes alcoholic, and is called hard cider. Unpasteurized cider (typically cider bought from fruit stands or directly from a small maker) will turn hard in a few weeks. Most cider sold in grocery stores is pasteurized and will not turn hard.

The basic process of cider making is the same no matter whether the maker is a small independent fruit grower or a large cider producer. The first step making cider is to choose the proper blend of apples.

Salary Range

Salaries for cider makers vary greatly, depending on the size of the operation, the location, and how and where the cider is marketed. The average earnings of a full-time cider maker working for a large facility range from $32,620 to $81,100. Many cider makers, especially those with small operations, rely on income from other ventures to supplement their cider-making income.

Education/Experience

There are no formal educational requirements to be a cider maker, and many people learn the trade by apprenticing. If you plan to grow the apples with which you'll make the cider and run a large operation, however, a degree in agriculture or a related area is recommended. Agricultural jobs are becoming increasingly complex and require business skills as well as agricultural knowledge. Some colleges and universities offer majors such as farm business management and finance, which combine agricultural courses with those in areas such as marketing, human resource management, finance, and strategic thinking.

Personal Attributes

A cider maker must be willing to work long hours during certain times of the year, and be able to deal with weather-related and other sorts of problems that occur. You should be easy to get along with and work well with people.

Requirements

Most states have requirements and standards concerning the production of apple cider, and efforts are underway to institute a national food safety standard for cider production. Most cider-making facilities need to be inspected and licensed.

Outlook

Jobs in all areas of food production are expected to increase by about 5 percent through 2012. Some areas, such as the production of organic foods, are expected to show a higher growth rate.

Mike Kurchak, cider maker

Mike Kurchak's cider-making operation is a small one, primarily developed to use extra apples from the orchards on his property. He also enjoys demonstrating to various groups how cider is made. Although Kurchak grew up on a farm, he had no intention of going into any sort of agricultural work.

"I went to engineering school so I wouldn't have to farm for a living," he explains. "But I found that it was hard to get away from. We bought a house in 1976 that had a few apple trees in back. Later, we bought more land next door and planted more apple trees. Now we have an orchard where people can come and pick their own apples and watch us make cider."

The cider maker's knowledge of the craft comes from extensive research and a lot of trial and error. "Learning to make cider is like learning to cook," he says. "Sometimes the first things you make aren't the best. The good part is that you can immediately taste your results, but sometimes it helps to have a nice chocolate chip cookie or donut to eat while you test the early batches."

Like most cider makers, Kurchak says that finding the right mix of apples is an all-important step. "The flavor of the cider definitely will depend on the variety of apples used," he says. "Some of the best apples for cider have been grown since Colonial times, when people drank cider as their beverage of choice."

Because Kurchak knows he can't make a living either making cider or selling apples at the small level on which he operates, he also works in the engineering field, using the cider and apple businesses as supplementary income. Large cider-making operations, however, can be a full-time business.

Kurchak, whose cider-making equipment is all hand operated, says he gets great satisfaction out of caring for the apple trees and seeing the fruit develop and eventually become cider. One thing he doesn't like about harvesting apples and making cider, however, is the frequency of bees. "The yellow jackets are the worst," he says. "I try not to get between them and the apples or the juice they're trying to get, but I usually get stung at least once every year."

When that happens, however, Kurchak has a home remedy that he swears by. "We try to keep fresh tomato leaves around to crush and put on the sting," he says. "It reduces the pain and swelling quite a bit—honest."

Most cider makers agree that good cider requires a mixture of sweet and tart apples, such as McIntosh, Granny Smith, Rome, Delicious, and Empire.

Finding the right apple varieties and determining which proportion of each should be used in the cider-making process can be a challenging and time-consuming job. While some cider makers develop their own recipes, others rely on those that have been handed down to them or otherwise obtained.

Once you've selected and obtained the apples you'll need, they need to be carefully sorted through, and any twigs or other debris removed. Apples that are rotten or have rotten spots should not be used.

The apples are then washed, either by hand or by using high-pressure water sprays. After that, they're put into a machine that grinds them up, and then into another machine that presses the apple grindings to extract the juice. In most cases, the juice is then pasteurized by heat or exposure to ultraviolet light to kill germs. Then it's bottled—either by hand or with an automated bottling system—or stored in tanks to be bottled later. The scope of cider-making equipment and the methods used to make cider vary greatly, depending on the size of the operation.

To produce hard cider, unpasteurized sweet cider is transferred into fermentation casks and allowed to ferment until the sugar in it has turned to alcohol.

A cider maker's job doesn't end, however, once the cider has been made and bottled. Being able to market your product is very important, as is keeping track of customers, orders, billing matters, and other business-related concerns. If you have a large cider-making operation, you'll have employees, vehicles to maintain and oversee, a manufacturing building that must be kept very clean, and other matters for which you'll be responsible.

Pitfalls

It's hard to make a good living out of a small cider-making business. The work is seasonal and labor intensive, and the profit margin is small. Because you must rely on apples to make the cider, you're subject to the same unpredictability of weather and other factors that plague farmers. You must learn and follow all regulations and standards concerning cider making, and adhere to strict sanitary guidelines. Severe cases of food-borne illness can result from unpasteurized or improperly handled cider.

Perks

People have been making and drinking cider for centuries, so it's an occupation with a long and varied tradition. Cider makers who still use the traditional methods of pressing apples by hand say they enjoy the satisfaction of seeing the rewards of their labors. Apple growers who make cider with apples that might otherwise go unused realize an economic benefit.

Get a Jump on the Job

If you know of a cider-making operation located near you, pay a visit and ask if you can watch the process. Some states have cider-making guilds or other organizations you may be able to join that offer education, information, and support to cider makers. Learn how to make your own apple cider (you don't need much equipment to make it in small quantities) and experiment with different blends of apples and different production processes. Learn all that you can about different kinds of apples and different methods of making cider.

COFFEE PURVEYOR

OVERVIEW

A coffee purveyor supplies coffee to businesses such as coffee shops, luncheonettes, hotels, and pastry shops. During the past 10 years or so, gourmet coffees have undergone a renaissance. The local diner with its giant urns brewing gallons of coffee at a time is no longer the place to grab a cup of joe and a donut. These days, there are all sorts of coffee options, including latte, cappuccino, and espresso, with foam, without foam, and more! They're available in chain coffee stores such as Starbucks, locally owned coffee shops, drive-through coffee shops, and boutique bakeries. Even your local convenience store is likely to serve various types and flavors of branded coffee. Coffee is big business, and it's expected to get even bigger in the next few years.

With so much coffee around, the job of a coffee purveyor has become more complicated, and much more important. Clients who used to be satisfied with one or two varieties of coffees now want a dozen or more. And as coffee drinkers have become more sophisticated, coffee purveyors must scramble to provide the best possible coffees in order to satisfy their tastes.

Coffee purveyors must have a sound knowledge of everything to do with the coffee they sell. They should know how and where it's grown, when it was harvested, roasting techniques for coffee and the difference between various types of coffee. Coffee purveyors are expected to be experts on coffee, so they can tell customers why one type is good or why another type might be better. They need to understand the processes by which coffees are flavored, and to be able to explain all these things to customers.

Just as wine is tasted, analyzed, and judged, so is coffee. And purveyors must not only know the ratings of different coffees, but must understand the process and the rationale through which the coffee received the ratings. Coffee purveyors must also know about different ways of preparing coffee and related beverages, such as espresso. Basically, a coffee purveyor must be able to serve as a valuable resource to customers, passing along knowledge and techniques, in addition to the coffee products.

Pitfalls

With coffee being such a hot commodity, there's a lot of competition among coffee purveyors. You might be expected to travel extensively to cover a large territory, and to work long hours in order to be accessible to clients. Any type of sales can be stressful as you work to meet quotas and please customers.

Perks

Coffee is trendy, and so are many of the people who own and run coffee shops and other coffee-related businesses. You're likely

Debra Dolan, coffee and specialty coffee equipment purveyor

Debra Dolan loves coffee. Five years ago, she opened a small café near her home in Mohnton, Pennsylvania, and has developed it into a thriving business. In her free time, she sells coffee and specialty equipment to customers in four states. "I think coffee is fascinating," she says. "It's a passion of mine."

Her fascination with coffee started when she discovered a small café where college students and professors gathered. It became her habit to sit in the café, drinking coffee and listening to the conversations around her. Gradually, she became increasingly interested in the coffee, and started reading and learning about it. Eventually, her strong interest in coffee motivated her to open her own café and get into the business of selling.

Dolan is more than a supplier of coffee and equipment, however. She serves as a consultant to her customers, walking them through how to operate and maintain the equipment, giving them hints on how best to prepare coffee and specialty drinks, and encouraging them in their business dealings.

Before Dolan opened her coffee business, she was highly motivated to learn all that she could about coffee. She studied its history, the roles it plays in various cultures, how it's grown, different types, and how it's best prepared. She attended trade shows, paying close attention to new innovations and products within the coffee industry. Now she encourages her customers to do the same.

"I want my customers to be educated," she says. "It's both in their interests and my interests to have them succeed. I'm always surprised how many people will get into a business without having learned what they need to know." And so, Dolan often finds herself to be not only a purveyor, but a coach, cheerleader, and teacher, as well.

(continues)

(continued)

Dolan knows a lot about coffee and the machines and accessories that accompany it. That's what allows her to work closely with her customers, helping them to set up their businesses and run them successfully, as she has her own business.

Although she greatly enjoys being in the coffee business, it involves a lot of traveling, hauling equipment and product, and being on call at all hours.

"If a customer runs into a problem that's related to something I sold him, you can bet that he's going to call and I'm going to have to figure out a way to solve the problem," Dolan says. "I always need to be ready to answer to customers."

Dolan is extremely interested in the continuing growth of the coffee craze in America, and sees her customer base spreading as more and more coffee shops and cafés open up. Her customers now include high-end restaurants and many coffee shops of varying sizes, located in places as diverse as day spas, commuter train stations, bagel shops, and a college library. She expects coffee shop locations to extend even further as consumers become more and more enamored.

"The coffee shop is still evolving, and it's going to be very interesting to see just how far it goes," Dolan says. "We'll be seeing more and more coffee shops in many different locations in the coming years."

As long as America's fascination with coffee continues, Dolan plans to continue selling coffee and related products. She is also educating herself about tea, which she says is becoming extremely popular on the West Coast.

Although her sales job at times becomes tedious, she says she thoroughly enjoys working with customers and helping them to succeed in their businesses. And, she says, the sales job allows her to spend many hours in good company—with coffee.

---

to meet some interesting people, and get to know the ins and outs of running a coffee business, as well as selling coffee. If you like meeting new people, sales work may be very appealing to you.

Get a Jump on the Job

Find out everything you can about coffee by visiting your local library and checking out the selections. Learn how it's grown, what the plants look like, and how it's roasted. Once you're old enough, you can apply for a job in a coffee shop or restaurant that serves specialty coffees, and learn how to make various drinks. Get familiar with different varieties of coffees and how they smell and taste.

COOKBOOK AUTHOR

OVERVIEW

Writing a cookbook is far more than just slapping together a collection of recipes with a few catchy titles. While there are cookbooks that are compilations of existing recipes (families, churches, civic organizations, and other groups often put together collections of recipes from members), the job of a cookbook author is to present new recipes in a fresh and appealing manner.

A cookbook may be comprehensive and include recipes for everything from appetizers to desserts, or may focus on just one area or type of cuisine. Some cookbooks are collections of ethnic or regional recipes, while others contain recipes intended for people with particular health concerns. In fact, there are cookbooks for just about every method of cooking imaginable and for nearly every type of food.

The average cookbook is about 350 pages long and contains about 150 recipes. Most require at least a year to develop, although it could take much longer for cookbook authors with other jobs.

Once you've decided to sit down and write a cookbook, you first have to come up with an idea or concept that sets it apart from the thousands of other cookbooks already available on crowded culinary bookshelves across America. You'll need to consider cooking and food trends, know the types of books that have already been published, and be able to communicate your ideas clearly to a publisher.

AT A GLANCE

Salary Range

Income for cookbook authors varies tremendously, depending on the type of book and its market, the celebrity status of the author, how many books the author writes, the publisher, agreements concerning royalties, and many other factors. A publisher could pay an advance ranging from a few thousand to many thousands of dollars for a cookbook. Nationwide, the average annual earnings for cookbook authors is about $43,000.

Education/Experience

Cookbook authors enter the business through different doors, but you'll need both culinary and writing training and experience. Ideally, you'll have a college degree in English, writing, communications, or a related field, in addition to culinary training and experience.

Personal Attributes

Writing a cookbook of original recipes requires patience and perseverance, as recipes must be tested and retested before they can be included. You should obviously have a strong interest in cooking and writing, and a good sense of the art and science necessary to be a successful cook. You must also be in tune with cooking trends, and able to communicate your ideas to readers and editors.

Requirements

You'll need a strong proposal to present to potential publishers, including a theme for the book, the recipes you plan to include, a marketing plan for the book, factors that make your cookbook different from others, and so forth.

Outlook

Writing jobs are expected to increase by between 10 and 20 percent through the year 2012. Jobs for cookbook authors are very competitive, although Web sites are providing additional opportunities.

Tish Boyle, cookbook author

Tish Boyle has published seven cookbooks and is working on another—yet she doesn't have the luxury of writing full time. That's because she's also the editor-in-chief of *Chocolatier* magazine and a food editor for *Pastry Art and Design* magazine. For that reason, it can take her as long as two years to see a cookbook through from start to finish. "It's a long process, to say the least," Boyle says.

Boyle has worked as a chef on a tourist barge in France, as a pastry chef at a Club Med resort, and as a caterer. She's cooked in restaurants, worked as a recipe developer and editor for *Good Housekeeping* magazine, and is known in the industry as a top-notch authority on baking. Still, even she runs up against a wall now and then when it comes to creating and writing her recipes.

"It doesn't always go the way you think it will, and then you have to be ready to change gears," she says. "I had a recipe that I tried to make about 10 times, and then I realized it just wasn't going to work. You have to be willing to accept failure occasionally."

Boyle has an English degree from Smith and received her culinary training at La Varenne École de Cuisine in Paris. The combination of writing and culinary training has contributed to her success as an editor and author, she says, allowing her to be able to present her ideas and recipes clearly and effectively.

Her cookbooks begin as ideas, followed by a lot of planning, testing, and writing. She has written *The Good Cookie, Diner Desserts, Chocolate Passion,* and *Simply Sensational Desserts,* all books written for home cooks. Her other cookbooks, *Grand Finales: A Neoclassic View of Plated Desserts, A Modernist View of Plated Desserts,* and *Grand Finales: The Art of the Plated Dessert,* are intended for professional pastry chefs.

It's extremely important, she says, to always remember the intended user of the book. "You always have to keep in mind who your audience is," Boyle says. "Pastry and desserts tend to be more difficult than savory recipes because there's a lot of chemistry involved. The recipes in

To do this, you create a proposal, providing a clear overview of what your book will include, how it's different from the competition (all those other cookbooks crowding the shelves of bookstores and libraries), who will want to read it (your target audience), and how it can be marketed. Then you need to add some sample recipes and include a list of all the recipes to be included in the book—actual recipes that have been carefully developed and tested—along with an idea of how they'd be organized and presented. You'll also need a section explaining your own expertise and why you're the best person to write this particular cookbook.

Most cookbook authors have extensive culinary experience, and are able to envision the results of a recipe in their heads. They know how flavors blend together, they have an idea of the amounts of ingredients that should be used, and they're familiar with the techniques necessary in cooking. Still, every recipe must be tested at least several times. And experienced chefs must be sure the books I've done for professionals are very complicated and difficult—much more so than the average person would want. But in the other books, I work hard to avoid recipes that are overly complicated or require special equipment or ingredients."

Boyle gets ideas for recipes by looking through magazines and cookbooks, and by thinking about different combinations of foods. "I'll get an idea for a specific combination of flavors or for pairing different textures, and I'll try it out," she says.

If she likes the combination, she develops a recipe around it, testing and re-testing as she goes. "I guess I test everything an average of four or five different times," she says. "Every now and then you get something down in one or two tries, but that doesn't happen very often."

So what does she do with all those test batches of cakes, pies, cookies, and pastries? "It's good to get them out of the house as soon as possible," Boyle says. "When I was working on the cookie book, my husband took all the cookies to his office. That was great because I could get some feedback from the people there."

Boyle's interest in cooking began early in her life, when she would cook at every chance. "My mother would let me make dinner, and my friend would come over and we would make these awful cakes," Boyle says. "I always cooked whenever I could." She grew up reading *Mastering the Art of French Cooking,* by the late, great chef Julia Child. "I used to pore over that book," Boyle says.

Reading cookbooks, which are available in nearly all libraries, is an excellent way to begin preparing to be a cookbook author, she says. So is watching food shows on TV and getting some hands-on experience in the kitchen.

"Start cooking as soon as you can, and educate yourself by reading cookbooks," she says. "Pay attention to what's happening with food by watching cooking shows and experiment a little bit when you cook. "The beautiful thing about cooking is that it's a great combination of art and science. It's meant to be creative."

that their recipes and cooking techniques aren't too difficult for the cookbook's target audience.

Once a cookbook is written and submitted to the publisher, it's painstakingly checked by an editor and copyeditor who understand both writing and cooking. The author is then responsible for reviewing the edits and responding to any questions or concerns of the editors.

As you can see, writing a cookbook isn't an easy task—and there's a lot of competition. However, there's just as much demand for more and more cookbooks. As food and cooking trends constantly change, new books are needed to fill the demand.

Pitfalls

Writing books can be a difficult field to break into, and you'll have all the typical headaches of the self-employed. Writing a cookbook is also extremely time-consuming, which means you could spend a year or more working on just one project.

Perks

If you love to cook and have a knack for putting together foods in unusual or new ways, what could be better than getting paid to develop, record, and test new recipes for others to use? Many writers—especially freelance writers—are able to set their own hours and have a degree of flexibility not found with all jobs.

Get a Jump on the Job

Get in the kitchen and cook as much as you can. Offer to help when others are cooking, and pay attention to what they're doing. Watch cooking shows on TV, check out recipes online, and read cookbooks to get an idea of how they're laid out and the elements they contain. Take home economics courses in high school and consider outside cooking classes offered in your community.

When you eat food that someone else has prepared, try to figure out what ingredients were used and notice how the flavors blend and complement one another. If you're old enough, consider getting a job in a restaurant or kitchen where you can watch trained chefs at work.

DAIRY FARMER

OVERVIEW

Dairy farmers typically own and operate family farms, although they may also lease additional land. Dairy farmers must feed and care for the animals and keep barns and other farm buildings clean and in good condition. They also plan and oversee breeding and marketing activities. But that's only a part of their work. Operators of small farms are usually masters of a number of jobs, including keeping records for management and tax purposes, servicing machinery, maintaining buildings, and growing hay, straw, and silage. The size of the farm often determines which of these tasks farmers handle themselves. Operators of larger dairy farms, on the other hand, have employees who help with the physical work that small farmers do themselves. Although employment on most small farms is limited to the farmer and one or two family workers or hired employees, some large farms have many more employees.

Dairy farming is strongly influenced by the weather, disease, fluctuations in milk prices, and federal farm programs. Most milk is sold to a milk cooperative. Farmers also negotiate with banks and other credit lenders to get the best financing deals for their equipment as well as their livestock and seed, and must keep track of changing prices. Just as in other businesses, dairy farming operations have become more complex, so many farmers use computers to log financial and inventory records, keep track of each cow's milk and cream output,

AT A GLANCE

Salary Range

Ranges from a low of $24,410 to a high of $81,100, with an average dairy farmer earning between $32,620 and $59,330. Incomes of farmers fluctuate because milk prices vary; however, government subsidies or other payments can supplement income and reduce some of the risk of farming.

Education/Experience

In the old days, you didn't need formal training to be a dairy farmer, although it helped to grow up on a dairy farm and inherit the business from your parents. Today a college degree in agriculture, agribusiness, or a related field is helpful to many young dairy farmers, although experience is still most important. Modern farming requires knowledge of new developments in agriculture, technology, genetics, and dairy science. Your high school training should include courses in mathematics, biology, and other life sciences. You also can complete a two-year degree or four-year degree program in a college of agriculture. In addition to formal education, you should spend time working for an experienced farmer in order to translate your academic training into practical skills.

Personal Attributes

Patience; ability to work hard; strength of character; ability to withstand stress; love of farming, animals, and the outdoors.

Requirements

Financial capability to run a farm, including feeding and caring for the dairy herd, and maintaining the barns, farm equipment, and milking machines. Mechanical aptitude and the ability to work with tools of all kinds are also valuable skills, since you'll be maintaining and repairing machinery and farm structures.

(continues)

AT A GLANCE (continued)

Outlook

Overall employment is projected to decline because of increasing productivity and consolidation of dairy farms. Market pressures and low prices for many agricultural goods will cause more dairy farms to go out of business through 2012. The complexity of modern farming and keen competition among farmers leaves little room for the marginally successful farmer. We'll always need milk, but it can be tough to earn a living as a dairy farmer; if you haven't inherited a farm, it is almost impossible to start out in the business. However, developments in organic farming are making small-scale dairy farming economically feasible again. Various government financial programs are available to help small farmers, and to help small farmers enlarge their business.

and handle databases and spreadsheets to manage breeding.

Many farmers have maintained their land for several generations, usually working from sunrise to sunset during the planting and harvesting seasons. During the rest of the year they plan next season's crops, market their output, and repair machinery; some may earn additional income by working a second job off the farm.

Animals, unless they are grazing, must be fed and watered every day, and dairy cows must be milked two or three times a day. Many dairy farmers monitor and attend to the health of their herds, which may include helping in the birthing of animals. Such farmers rarely get the chance to get away unless they hire an assistant or arrange for a temporary substitute.

Even if you've grown up on a farm, modern farming requires increasingly complex scientific, business, and financial decisions, so you should think seriously

about college. In the United States, all state university systems have one land-grant university with a school of agriculture, offering courses in agronomy, dairy science, agricultural economics and business, crop science, and animal science. The college curriculum should include courses in agricultural production, marketing, and economics.

You'll also need to keep up with advances in agricultural methods, as well as changes in governmental regulations that may impact your dairy. The Internet allows quick access to the latest developments in areas such as agricultural marketing, legal arrangements, growing crops, and livestock. A basic knowledge of veterinary science and animal husbandry is also important.

But operating a dairy farm is more than just knowing how to milk cows and keep your equipment in good working order. Farmers need the managerial skills necessary to organize and operate a business, including a basic knowledge of accounting and bookkeeping, while knowledge of credit sources is vital for buying seed, fertilizer, and other inputs necessary for planting. It's also necessary to understand the complex regulations and requirements of governmental agricultural support programs. Computer skills are increasingly important, especially on large farms, where computers are widely used for recordkeeping and business analysis.

Despite the expected continued consolidation of farmland and the projected drop in dairy farms, more and more small-scale farmers have developed successful market niches involving personal contact with customers. Many are finding opportunities in organic dairy foods, as more consumers demand milk and dairy products produced without chemicals, hormones, or antibiotics. Farmers' markets

Bob Selleck Jr., dairy farmer

For more than 130 years, the rolling dairy pastureland in northern Pennsylvania has been farmed by a succession of Sellecks: Bob, his father, his father's father, and so on, back in an unbroken chain to the earliest dark-haired Welsh Selleck who first took plow to field. A legacy like this means that managing the dairy herd is not a job but a heritage, and makes it all the more difficult to keep together in this time of shrinking profits and growing costs.

Selleck works the farm with his younger brother Jeff. The farm's 70 milking cows support both of their families and their father, Robert Sr. But dairy farming isn't just about milking cows, he notes. "It also involves lots of mechanical work, fixing the machines, and breeding—we breed our own cows. I love the genetics, and I love the outdoors." The pitfall, he says, is that a dairy farmer doesn't get a day off. "You have to be there twice a day to milk, including Christmas, holidays—it creates a problem sometimes. You don't get your vacations when you have a small farm, and you don't have a hired man."

Selleck and his wife Edith have raised two sons on the farm, both of whom have left the business (one to teach, the other to work as an engineer). While his father spent time and money improving the buildings and adding land, Bob Junior chose to focus his efforts on improving the herd.

"I love the independence, being your own boss," he says, "and the variety and opportunities to do different things."

that cater directly to urban and suburban consumers allow the farmers to capture a greater share of consumers' food dollars. Some small-scale dairy farmers belong to collectively owned marketing cooperatives that process and sell their product. Other farmers participate in community-supported agriculture cooperatives that allow consumers to directly buy a share of the farmer's milk.

Pitfalls

Dairy farmers work incredibly long hours, seven days a week, 365 days a year. Cows need to be milked at least twice a day—whether you're sick, not feeling like it, or want to take a vacation. Farm work can also be hazardous. Tractors and other farm machinery can cause serious injury, and workers must be constantly alert on the job. In addition, chemicals used during crop production can be toxic.

Perks

Although farming consists of hard work, long hours, and rare days off during the planting, growing, and harvesting seasons, most dairy farmers would tell you that the disadvantages are outweighed by the quality of life in a rural area, working outdoors, being self-employed, and making a living working the land.

Get a Jump on the Job

Start out now working on a dairy farm to see if you like the hard work and various duties; you can work after school or during the summers. Try participating in agricultural programs for kids sponsored by the National FFA Organization (formerly known as the Future Farmers of America), the 4-H youth educational programs, or other educational opportunities offered by the Extension Service.

DOG BISCUIT CHEF

OVERVIEW

In the old days, the family dog was perfectly happy with a bowl of basic dog food plopped from a can—the no-frills method of feeding a pet. But today, as people get more finicky about their own food, they've also become more health conscious when it comes to Fido and Fi-Fi. More and more pooch lovers have decided to take advantage of this concern by starting their own dog bakeries, offering healthy treats to lucky canines. They point out that commercial dog biscuits are filled with additives and chemicals, and that home-baked goodies sidestep all that unnecessary stuff. What's more, dogs seem to love them.

Dog biscuit chefs typically start their companies right in their own homes, using ingredients from the corner grocery store to whip up dog treats on their own stoves. This translates into lower production costs and a healthier bottom line. Once the goodies are baked, the biscuit chef packages them in a variety of attractive ways (anything from Brown Paper Bag Basic to fancy shrink-wrapped biscuit-filled tins, dog bowls, or baskets).

Then it's off with the production hat and on with the marketing chapeau, as the biscuit chef must now figure out how to get the treats to buyers. Often, the chef can start with local pet stores, vets' offices, and kennels. They may set up a Web site and start selling through the mail, or come up with a mail-order catalog. Some

limit their wares to wholesale, while others scout out a storefront and sell their product themselves. (This requires quite a bit of an investment, not to mention business savvy.)

Pitfalls

You've got to have a head for business in this job, and you'll have to make sure it's legal to prepare and sell dog food from your home (laws will vary from area to area). Once you become successful, you reach that difficult stage where you must decide what to do yourself and what duties to delegate. Most specialty pet food chefs don't have formal cooking training,

Daryl Ostrovsky, dog biscuit chef

Daryl Ostrovsky is that rarity in the pet food biz—an award-winning chef who got into the dog biscuit business from a technical cooking background, rather than just being a pet owner who loves pooches.

He started out, as many kids do, with dreams of becoming a vet. When he realized how much schooling he'd need, he changed course, and veered off into the food business—the human food business.

The idea to start a dog bakery really began when Ostrovsky was living in Atlanta with his one-year-old dog Cosmo, and attending the School of Culinary Arts there. "Going to chef's school, I became fascinated with reading labels, understanding all the types of ingredients that were in foods," he recalls. "In looking for treats for Cosmo, I noticed that there were more and more companies in this type of business. As good as some of these treats were, I knew I could make something that tasted better and was substantially healthier."

After graduating from culinary school, he started working as chef at various Atlanta restaurants, including a stint as a pastry chef. He finally decided to take the dog food plunge after he realized that running a restaurant was a lot of work with not much reward. "I was working crazy hours, and not having any fun," he says.

After he tested a few recipes, his first finished "recipe" was the peanut butter biscuit (a canine favorite), now called "Cosmo's Biscuits." He soon expanded the line to include chicken, ginger, and mint biscuits.

Then came an opportunity to open a bakery and small retail store just for dogs in Portland; Cosmo and Ostrovsky moved there, and the Great Dog Bakery opened its doors in March 2001. "The best part of this job is that my dog gets to work with me," he says. "He didn't do well when he was left by himself. The best part is watching the dogs enjoy my biscuits."

There are a lot of homemade dog food biscuit chefs out there, but Ostrovsky suspects he's one of the very few (and maybe the only one) professionally trained as a chef. He makes sure he uses only the finest and freshest quality ingredients, free of preservatives and artificial additives, and his biscuits are baked fresh to order.

"My great dog Cosmo is my resident taste-tester and I offer nothing to my customers that hasn't gotten his personal stamp of approval," he says. "I'm not knocking the other companies, but nobody uses the ingredients I use. I won't buy frozen chicken. I buy fresh skinless boneless chicken breasts and remove all the fat. Then I freeze the chicken and use it in my biscuits."

The Great Dog Bakery sells its biscuits online, at dog shows, and is currently negotiating to sell its products in Amsterdam. "I'm happy to sell my dog biscuits anywhere it's legal to do so," he says. With the launching of his Web site, his treats are now available to dog lovers everywhere. "I'm living my dream of doing something with and for dogs," he says.

To make your own dog treats, try this recipe for Cool Banana Pupsicles from the Great Dog Bakery: Mix two cups of vanilla yogurt, four bananas (mashed), and two tablespoons of honey, and freeze in an ice cube tray. Makes about two ice cube trays.

although the few who do have that much more chance of success.

Perks

If you love dogs, love cooking, and dream of running your own business, what could be a better way to employ your talents? Dog biscuit chefs who also have a storefront have the added fun of actually seeing dogs enjoying their biscuits. And because the specialty pet food market is booming, there are more and more opportunities to design your own pet treats and set up your own business, either from a storefront or via mail order.

Get a Jump on the Job

Start reading as much as you can about healthy foods for dogs. Try getting a job at a kennel or at the vet's office to learn as much as you can about canine nutrition. Also try learning as much as you can about cooking and about running a business.

FAST FOOD FRANCHISEE

OVERVIEW

When you see a McDonald's, Kentucky Fried Chicken, Wendy's, or Taco Bell restaurant, it's a pretty good bet that the restaurant is owned and operated by an individual. These restaurants are called franchises. The people who own them are called franchisees.

There are lots of businesses that franchise, such as Pearle Vision, Dunkin Donuts, Pizza Hut, and Merry Maids. When you buy a franchise, you're buying into the proven name and reputation of the business and its managerial formula.

Different corporations have different franchise requirements. All of them require that you pay an up-front fee called a franchise fee. McDonald's, for instance, requires an initial franchise fee of $45,000. That, however, is not the only cost involved, and costs are ongoing. You'll need in the ballpark of anywhere between $500,000 and $1 million to set yourself up in a McDonald's franchise.

Once your franchise is up and running, you'll be required to pay McDonald's a monthly fee of 4 percent of your sales, plus rent. You see, McDonald's is not only a hamburger joint. It's also got a huge real estate component, because it owns the land on which all its restaurants is located. The franchisee may own the building, but McDonald's owns the land.

As you can see, getting a fast-food franchise can require big bucks. And you'll

AT A GLANCE

Salary Range
Varies considerably depending on location, size of restaurant, number of franchises owned, and so on, but a profitable location could earn the franchisee more than $100,000 a year.

Education/Experience
There are no set educational requirements to become a franchisee, but McDonald's, for example, won't grant a franchise to someone who doesn't have business experience. At least a two-year associate degree in a business program is recommended, as well as some practical business experience.

Personal Attributes
You should have good business sense, be able to manage, motivate, and lead workers, and have good communication skills because you'll be working closely with representatives of the chain. Running a business also requires patience, the ability to solve problems, and flexibility.

Requirements
Requirements vary, depending on the chain. You'll need to pay a franchise fee ranging from $15,000 to more than $50,000. In addition, you'll need a minimum amount of capital.

Outlook
Good. Fast-food chains are an established part of the American landscape, with more opening all the time.

be required to follow all of the corporation's rules regarding quality, service, inventory control, employment, appearance of the restaurant, and more.

McDonald's, Kentucky Fried Chicken, and Taco Bell are household names, so when you buy one of these franchises, you're buying instant recognition. You'll be required to participate in a corporate-

George Skylass, McDonald's franchisee

George Skylass has been a McDonald's franchisee since 1980, when his father-in-law invited him to join him in business. Today, Sklyass has six McDonald's restaurants in southeastern Pennsylvania, and spends his time traveling between them, playing an active role in how the restaurants are operated. "Obviously, I can't be in six restaurants at the same time, but I'm very hands-on with all of them," Skylass says. "McDonald's doesn't want any absentee ownership. They're looking for hands-on management."

Getting a McDonald's franchise is no small task, Skylass says, sometimes taking years before everything is in place and you're up and running.

The first thing you need to do is file a lengthy and detailed application with the McDonald's corporation, stating your preference for a location and providing financial information and background information pertaining to your ability to run a business. If the corporation thinks you have potential as a franchisee, it will contact you and set up a time for an interview.

If corporate representatives are impressed at the interview, you might be granted status as a registered applicant. Even that, however, doesn't mean you are going to end up with a restaurant to call your own.

Registered applicants must work for a required time at another McDonald's restaurant, putting in a specified number of hours and undergoing specialized McDonald's training.

"It's very difficult and time consuming," Skylass says. "It's not a sure thing at all. You don't know whether you're going to be approved or not until they actually award you a store."

And then, of course, Skylass says, you become financially responsible for the restaurant, which may or may not be located in the area that you requested.

"You've got to be ready to pick up and go to where a store is available," Skylass says.

run training program, during which time you learn the ins and outs of running a franchise. The corporation with which you're franchising should provide continued support once your restaurant is up and running, handling all advertising.

Statistically, buying and running a franchise is less risky than starting your own business from scratch; you're more likely to succeed with an established chain restaurant than by starting your own burger joint.

As you can see, there are advantages and disadvantages to being a franchisee. Overall, opportunities are good for

franchise owners who are willing to work hard to keep the business on track.

Pitfalls

Most people don't have half a million dollars sitting in a checking account, ready to hand over to a fast-food corporation. Of course, you can borrow money to get started, but most chains require that a certain percentage of your start-up money is not borrowed. As with any business that you own, there can be unanticipated expenses such as leaky roofs, faulty equipment, and so forth. Running a restaurant typically entails managing the staff, so you'll either need to be prepared

McDonald's has very clear operating procedures, and franchise owners are expected to follow them. On the other hand, Skylass says, corporate officials know that it is in the best interests of the corporation to have its franchisees succeed, and are willing to work with store owners to help them achieve their goals.

Once you own a McDonald's franchise, it may or may not be easier to get a second one, Skylass says.

If you've proven yourself by having a franchise that's very successful, company officials will probably be more likely to consider you for a second location. However, Skylass says, they also want to protect you from getting in over your head or overextending yourself financially, so they will carefully consider various factors before making a decision.

While Skylass acknowledges the many regulations and restrictions involved with owning McDonald's franchises, he also says that the businesses can be lucrative if they're carefully managed.

With about 500 employees in his six restaurants, Skylass spends a great deal of time tending to staffing issues. It's important, he says, to maintain a steady number of employees, which means he's always hiring and training new people to replace those who leave.

Skylass recommends that anyone interested in becoming a McDonald's franchisee begins by working at one of its restaurants and learning the ins and outs of the business. You need a significant amount of money in order to get a restaurant up and running, so you'll need to consider that aspect, as well, Skylass says.

All in all, he says, being a McDonald's franchisee has been a good business venture for him, and he finds his work to be enjoyable.

to deal with all types of people or have a dependable manager to do so.

Perks

Depending on their locations and other factors, fast-food restaurants can be extremely lucrative, so your investment may pay off handsomely. Many people are attracted to franchising because of the decreased business risk and increased chance for success.

Get a Jump on the Job

It can't hurt to learn about chain restaurants from the ground up, so getting a job at your local chain might just be the best way to get started. Talk to the manager, or the franchisee, is he or she is available. Check out the U.S. Small Business Administration at http://www.sba.gov to find out more about franchising, and read books about starting and running a business.

FISH PURVEYOR

OVERVIEW

The fish you see neatly lined up at the supermarket seafood counter didn't just get there by accident. Most likely, a fish purveyor was involved somewhere along the way. A fish purveyor (sometimes called a fishmonger) is someone who deals in the buying and selling of fish. He or she might buy directly from fishermen and resell to wholesale and retail fish sellers, restaurants and hotels, grocery stores, or specialty shops. Some fish purveyors own their own retail shops in which they resell the fish they've bought. Fish purveyors also may buy fish from large, wholesale fish markets, such as the Fulton Fish Market in New York City, the Pike Place Fish Market in Seattle, or Trang's Seafood Market in San Diego.

A fish purveyor might process fish to meet the specifications of customers by boning it or cutting it into filets or steaks. Other fish purveyors buy the fish already processed and resell it as is. Regardless of how much you handle the fish, or who eventually gets the fish you acquire, you need to know a lot about fish and seafood in order to be sure you're getting a good quality product at a fair price. If you provide a fish that ends up making customers sick, you could be looking at some legal problems. In short, it's imperative that you know what to look for to assure that the fish you buy is as fresh and desirable as possible.

While knowing how to buy fish is vitally important to a fish purveyor, it is equally important to know how to sell it.

Ed Stauffer, fish purveyor

Ed Stauffer has some nice childhood memories of fishing from his dad's boat, enjoying both the company of his father and the thrill of the catch. But he never imagined that one day seafood would become both his passion and his livelihood. "I always liked to eat seafood. I guess maybe that's why I got into it," says Stauffer, who owned his own seafood business for 25 years.

His multifaceted business kept him occupied seven days a week during busy seasons. In addition to paying weekly visits to East Coast fish markets to buy fish for resale in his own store, Stauffer also provided fish to local restaurants, ran a catering business, taught sushi classes, and operated a second retail location in a nearby farmer's market.

On Mondays, when his retail store was closed, he figured out what fish and seafood he'd need, placed orders, booked catering jobs and sushi classes, checked in with clients, and caught up with his business. There were always bills to pay, invoices to send out, employee paychecks to be signed, and so forth. On Tuesdays, Stauffer made his weekly trip to a major seafood market in New York, Philadelphia, or Maryland to see what was available and to buy some of the fish he'd sell in his store or provide to area restaurants. He bought the rest of the fish from fisherman and fish dealers in other locations, most of whom he worked with for years. Wednesday through Friday, he kept busy overseeing the two retail operations, checking out deliveries, hiring and training employees, placing newspaper ads for specials, and advising customers on the best methods of preparing the fish or seafood they buy.

Stauffer had catering jobs to tend to nearly every Friday and Saturday night in the summer and during holiday periods, all of which he did himself, aided by a small staff. "Sometimes it seemed like there aren't enough hours in the day, but I like keeping busy," he says. "I have a lot of energy, I guess."

Stauffer's business operated smoothly most of the time, which he credits to the contacts he has worked hard over the years to develop. "If you're going to be in this business, you've got to have contacts that you can rely on," Stauffer says. "And you've got to earn those contacts. They don't just happen."

When you have customers demanding certain items, it's nice to be able to make a call to someone you know to find out where you can get the product you need, he says.

"You have to have good sources," Stauffer says. "If you want to get what you need and get it in a timely manner, you have to be able to pick up the phone and call someone you can trust."

When buying fish, he says, it's important to discuss what's available, its quality, and its cost. There can be a big difference in fish, Stauffer says, even when it comes off the same boat. "Fishing boats might be out for a week or even 10 days," he says. "So think about the fish that are caught the first day. They get thrown into the bottom of the box, and all the other fish get thrown in on top of them. By the time the boat gets back, some of those fish are already 10 days old."

In that case, he says, it's important to have the right contacts so that you can get the freshest fish off the boat. And it's very important to listen to someone talk about the quality of fish,

(continues)

(continued)

especially if you're ordering fish over the phone. "You have to try to hear the voice and know what they're doing," Stauffer says. "If you ask somebody about the quality of the tuna, there's a big difference in whether they say: 'They're okay,' or if they say: 'Oh, they're like diamonds jumping out of the water.'"

Even when you're assured that you're getting the best quality fish available, ordering can be a tricky proposition. "You practically need a Ouija board to know how much of everything to buy," Stauffer says. "One day you can't stock enough of a certain fish, and the next week it sits in the case and nobody buys it."

Plus, he says, supplies are affected by wind and other weather, causing prices to fluctuate greatly. "Flounder might cost four or five dollars a pound one week, then go to eight dollars a pound the next," he says. "Then I have to ask myself how much I think my customers will be willing to pay. If something goes out of sight for price, I usually back off and wait until it's more reasonable. You really have to be on top of things because the prices change so much."

Stauffer spent a lot of time preparing food to sell in his store and at the farmer's market location. Customers bought ready-to-eat fish sandwiches; cooked shrimp, crabs, and lobsters; prepared salads; various varieties of sushi; crusted fish ready to pop into the oven; and a host of other freshly prepared, convenient options. "That seems to be the trend," he says. "People want something that's all ready for them to use."

If you're thinking of going into the seafood business, Stauffer says, it's important to make sure you're in an area that can support you. Seafood tends to be expensive and sells better in areas where people are reasonably affluent. People in less affluent areas may still buy fish, but they tend to buy whole fish that they clean and prepare themselves, resulting in little profit for the purveyor. "You really want to be in an area that has a certain level of income, because seafood is a high-cost product," Stauffer says.

And, he says, you need to be willing to work hard to get the best product available, be able to sell it at a fair price, and set yourself apart from other fish purveyors. "My favorite motto is that you either have to be better or be cheaper in order to get ahead," Stauffer says. "And I chose to be better."

You must be very familiar with the wants and needs of your customers in order to provide the products they want. A great buy on a load of rock fish isn't really a great buy if none of your customers can stand the stuff.

How you'll distribute the fish is another important factor to consider. Because fish is fragile and highly perishable, you'll need to have a refrigerated truck to transport it to buyers. If you pay someone else to transport it, you'll need to be sure the truck used is at the proper temperature and the conditions are sanitary.

A fish purveyor must be diplomatic and know how to deal with customers who sooner or later are bound to be disappointed because a certain fish they wanted was not available, or cost more than what they wanted to pay. Fish availability varies greatly depending on weather and other factors, and you need to be able to work with clients who have specific wants and needs.

Pitfalls

The buying and selling of fish begins before the sun comes up, so if you're the sort of person who likes to work on a traditional schedule, that could be a problem. Because fishing is unpredictable, thereby making for unpredictable supplies, you're bound to run into occasional problems filling orders and meeting demands.

Perks

Purveying fish involves extensive dealing with many different people, and you tend to meet some characters when you're hanging out at a fish market in the middle of the night. It's exciting to find a really great fish and be able to pass it along to a customer, especially if you get it at a good price. Many fish purveyors enjoy the thrill of the hunt for the perfect fish.

Get a Jump on the Job

Learn all that you can about fish and seafood. Find out where different varieties of fish come from, how they're caught, and how they should be stored and prepared. If possible, go out on a fishing boat to see firsthand how fish are caught. It doesn't have to be a commercial boat. Even a personal boat or a head boat (a boat where each person pays to fish and all equipment usually is provided) will give you a glimpse of the fishing process.

Visit fish markets or fish stores—even the fish counter in your grocery store can be informative—and ask where and when the fish was caught, if it's ever been frozen, how it should be prepared, and whatever else comes to mind. Be inquisitive about fish and explore any avenue you can think of to learn more. When you are old enough, you could get a job in a fish store or the seafood department of a grocery store to learn even more.

FLAIR BARTENDER

OVERVIEW

All good bartenders can mix cocktails, pour drinks, take food orders, wipe up the bar, and make customers feel comfortable. Flair bartenders take their jobs quite a bit further. If you notice liquor bottles flipping through the air, several bottles pouring at once, and all sorts of sleight of hand going on up at the bar, it's safe to say some flair bartending is going on.

Every flair bartender is different, but some practices you're likely to see include performing magic tricks, flipping bottles or glasses, doing tricks with drink garnishes, pouring from multiple bottles at a time, and seamlessly cracking jokes while mixing drinks. Flair bartenders seek to entertain as well as serve their guests.

Flair bartending (also known as extreme bartending) is a fast-growing field, and a practice that's becoming popular in restaurants across the country. As the job gets more popular, more and more bartenders are signing up for classes and looking for restaurants and bars that will let them perform while they work. Some chain restaurants, such as TGI Friday's and Smokey Bones, hire flair bartenders, as do lavish hotel bars in Las Vegas. Other cities with a big flair presence include Chicago, Orlando, Tampa, and London. But the trend toward flair, however, is cropping up in bars everywhere.

Basically, there are two categories of flair bartending: working flair and exhibition flair. Working flair, according

AT A GLANCE

Salary Range

While a regular bartender can expect to earn between $8 and $10 an hour, plus tips, a really good flair bartender—someone who can flip glassware and do lots of pouring tricks—working in a major city like Chicago can earn $100,000 a year. An accomplished flair bartender working in Las Vegas—known as the Flair Capital of the World—can make as much as $200,000 a year.

Education/Experience

There are no educational requirements to become a flair bartender, but there are schools that teach flair bartending. You can find them listed online.

Personal Attributes

Flair bartending involves flipping bottles and glassware, pouring from two or three bottles at a time, and other tricks, so you'll need to have excellent hand-eye coordination. You must also be personable, able to talk easily with customers and make them feel at home, and know enough about what's going on in the world to be informed and interesting. You should have a neat appearance and be well groomed.

Requirements

If you want to work in Las Vegas, you'll need to be certified as a Level 3 bartender. That's because most people in the hospitality industry in Las Vegas work under union contracts. Anywhere else, you'll just need to be good at what you do, and of legal age to serve liquor in your state.

Outlook

Excellent. Flair bartending is catching on in major cities across the country, with an industry building to support it. While flair bartending was really just a concept in the late 1990s, today there are flair bartending schools, equipment suppliers, and flair bartending competitions in cities around the world.

Robert Taylor, flair bartender

Robert Taylor was waiting tables at a TGI Friday's restaurant when he noticed a bartender flipping bottles and performing other tricks behind the bar. Right away, Taylor was hooked. "I knew then and there that was what I wanted to do," he says.

Taylor threw his heart into learning flair bartending, and began to develop a reputation as being skilled at what he did. He was hired by Darden Restaurants Inc., the company that owns and operates the Red Lobster, Olive Garden, Bahama Breeze, and Smokey Bones chains, to train flair bartenders in 25 new restaurants.

Even as he was training other bartenders in the art of flair, however, Taylor knew he had a lot more to learn.

"It was during the time we were opening those new restaurants that I realized how much more I had to learn," Taylor says. "I caught a special on flair bartending competitions in Vegas and was amazed at what those guys were doing."

He joined the Flair Bartenders Association (see Appendix A for more information) and began entering all the competitions he could get to. As his skills continued to improve, his passion for flair bartending also grew.

At the end of 2003, Taylor decided he wanted to run a flair bartending competition. Needing a business entity to attract sponsors for the competition, he formed a company called Bartrix. Before he knew it, Bartrix took off, in the next year sponsoring six more competitions, judging competitions in seven different states, and conducting countless flair bartending training programs.

Taylor even produced a flair bartender calendar called Bartenders and Beauties, and was called on to be the keynote speaker at the flair bartending convention in Puebla, Mexico.

"Who would have thought where this thing would lead me?" Taylor mused. "I've been able to take something fun, that I love to do, and build a company from it. I've been to Mexico, am scheduled to judge a competition in Costa Rica, and have had two all-expenses-paid trips to Europe, all because I am passionate about flair bartending."

While running Bartrix keeps Taylor pretty busy, he still tends bar on weekends, just because he wants to.

"I make a decent amount of money running Bartrix, but I still love going in for my two bartending shifts a week," Taylor says.

Sheer enjoyment of the job, he says, is a trait common to most professional flair bartenders, even those who compete in and promote the competitive events. "Pretty much all of the competing bartenders also tend bar," Taylor says. "Some of them compete more than others, but most of them also work behind the bar. Even most of the event promoters work a few bartending shifts. You'll find that most flair bartenders do it for the pure fact that they completely love it."

Flair bartenders are known not only for their showmanship but also for having excellent bartending skills. Taylor attributes that to the fact that many of them are constantly refining their

(continues)

(continued)

bartending skills while training for competitions. Popular competition categories are in speed and accuracy, which means flair bartenders are always working on those skills.

"While you prepare yourself for the competitions, it only makes you better in your job," he says. "You'll find that flair bartenders also are some of the most accurate and fastest bartenders in the business."

Taylor predicts that before too long, nearly all bartenders will be expected to practice some degree of flair bartending. "I think that eventually, flair will be another necessary skill required to get a job," he says. "Maybe not at all places, but I think flair is going to have a big influence on the bartending industry in the years to come. "

Flair bartending is starting to show up on television shows such as *The Ellen Show* and *The Ron White Show*, and on food and travel shows. The Flair Bartending Association has provided a home for bartenders, allowing them to share information about competitions, jobs, and techniques, and giving greater legitimacy to flair bartending as a profession. And, Taylor says, there are more and more competitions all the time. "Flair bartending has just grown tremendously over the past three years" he says. "It's been pretty amazing to see."

He encourages anyone who's interested in becoming a flair bartender to be willing to work hard in order to excel at the job. "It's really all about practice and dedication," he says. "You get out of it what you put into it. Some people might only practice a couple of hours a week, but the world champions are practicing as much as 10 hours a day."

As for himself, he plans to continue working, running his business, and practicing his flair bartending skills. "This is a great job," Taylor says. "I have made great friends all over the world, and there's never a dull moment."

to the Flair Bartender's Association, involves light, speedy, realistic moves that can be performed without slowing down service. Working flair is recommended for regular bar shifts, and it's only performed during the actual act of mixing drinks. Flipping bottles just for the heck of it isn't considered working flair, and it's not encouraged by the Flair Bartender's Association.

Exhibition flair, on the other hand, is performed expressly for entertainment or competitive purposes. Exhibition flair routines can be complicated, involving special preparation with bottle and prop set-ups. According to the Flair Bartender's Association, exhibition flair doesn't lend itself to everyday bar shifts; instead, the special moves should be reserved for exhibition and competition. Unlike working flair, exhibition flair is not restricted to the drink-making process, but can be performed solely for entertainment.

Once a flair bartender has become accomplished, he or she can enter competitions on the local, regional, national, and international levels. (Most flair bartenders are men, but there are some women in the profession.)

Some of the major competitions include the Grand Cayman Masters, the Tampa Showcase, the Southern New England Bartender Challenge, the Roadhouse Flair

Challenge, the Big Apple Showdown, King of the Ring, Pinnacle of Bartending, Cali's Best Bartender, and the Southern Classic Competition. Bartenders compete at different levels and can win prize money in these competitions.

Most bartenders can teach themselves a couple of tricks, but that doesn't qualify them as flair bartenders. While flair bartenders don't officially need any training, they should be familiar with the concepts of flair bartending and understand the expectations associated with the job. Professionals take their work seriously, and are resentful of bartenders who present themselves as flair bartenders while actually just showing off for customers.

The only way to get good at flair bartending, according to the experts, is to practice. A serious flair bartender working toward a competition might practice six to eight hours a day. While some flair bartenders like to practice with someone who has more experience, it's important to develop your own style of bartending, and not just copy what someone else is doing.

Pitfalls

Bartending of any kind, including flair bartending, tends to involve working long, irregular hours, with unpredictable results. You might be expecting a busy Saturday night with lots of tips, and end up with a practically empty bar and equally empty pockets.

In addition, some drinking establishments still contain unhealthy levels of smoke, although some municipalities and states have banned smoking in bars, and today many tavern owners provide better ventilation than in the past.

Perks

Flair bartending is fun, according to those who do it. Flair bartenders normally get more and bigger tips than traditional bartenders. In the right market, you can make good money. Flair bartenders get to socialize while they work, entertain their customers, and work in a generally upbeat atmosphere. According to one flair bartender, when you're in the profession, going to work isn't really work at all.

Get a Jump on the Job

The only way to learn flair bartending is to practice it. It's highly recommended, however, that if you're going to practice tossing and flipping bottles, you use plastic. Go online and look for videos and instructions for flair bartending tricks, and read books about bartending. (See the "Read All About It" section at the back of this book.) The Flair School, an online site located at http://www.theflairschool.com, offers free, basic online flair training and flair bartending tutorials.

FOOD PACKAGE DESIGNER

OVERVIEW

What beverage is sold in bright red-and-white cans? What chocolate product comes in a brown and white convex tin? What salt is sold in dark blue cylinders with a girl carrying an umbrella on the front? Odds are, you can answer each and every one of those questions, because well-known foods are typically packaged in easily recognizable containers. The dream of the food company is that when you think of their product, their distinctive package instantly comes to mind.

Of course, there's more to a package than just providing conveyance for a food product—the package must also help sell the item and protect it. The job of a package designer is to create an eye-catching package that's economical to produce. But you can't just sit down and come up with a pretty picture and some attractive words; the package must be highly focused so that it can communicate positively to the consumer, while meeting the specific needs of specific people. A package designer must think about the kind of consumer the package is trying to attract. (Are you aiming for a young, hip market? Or an older, more settled buyer?) In addition, the designer must understand what the brand stands for and what emotional reaction the company wants to trigger. Does the company stand for down-home goodness, big-city sophistication, just-like-Mom-used-to-make, or edgy Asian fusion?

AT A GLANCE

Salary Range

Starting salary is about $21,500; after 5 to 10 years, salary can range from $36,500 to more than $75,000 depending on whether you work for a company or own your own design firm.

Education/Experience

Although a bachelor's degree is not required to become a food packaging designer, most do go to college and major in art, product design, or art history. Coursework should include design, drawing, and computer artwork. There are more than 100 accredited graphic design programs.

Personal Attributes

Artistic ability, technological artistry, and ability to meet deadlines, sizing limits, and financial restrictions.

Requirements

Should be familiar with computer technology such as Adobe PageMaker, Photoshop, Adobe Illustrator, and other painting or graphic design tools.

Outlook

Excellent. There will continue to be a need for creative, innovative food packagers.

Further, if the product comes in different sizes or flavors, you've got to come up with a way to highlight those differences, while keeping in mind where and how the product will be sold. In the end, the better your up-front research is, the more successful the package design will be.

Most food package designers become in-house consultants, designers, and producers; only about 10 percent remain independent freelance designers.

Louise Fili, food package designer

Growing up in an Italian home, food was a constant topic at the family table, but art was also an interest of Louise Fili's. After college, she landed a job as a senior designer for Herb Lubalin and then went on to become an award-winning art director of Pantheon books, where she designed more than 2,000 book jackets. In addition to her design work, she has taught graphic design and typography and was inducted into the Art Directors Hall of Fame.

"I was an art director of Pantheon Books for 11 years," Fili explains. "When I started out, book jackets were all following the same tired formula. I set out to prove that a jacket didn't need to shout to attract a buyer's attention; that quiet elegance could be just as powerful. After I achieved this in book publishing, I decided to try to do the same for restaurants and food packaging."

Fili began her own company designing food packages, restaurant logos, and book jackets in 1989 (Louise Fili Ltd.). One of her first jobs was to design a package for The El Paso Chile Company's margarita mix and salt, to be sold through Williams-Sonoma. After discovering the work of nineteenth-century Mexican woodcut artist José Guadalupe Posada, she gave a sketch to a wood engraver, who created a delicate woodcut of cactus and limes. She combined that with her hand-drawn lettering to produce the bottle's label.

"The design of food packages can often have many commercial constraints, but it can still afford some lively experimentation," she says. "And, unlike restaurants, food packages tend to stay around longer. I love to walk into a store and see packages that I have designed."

Fili also travels to Italy and France on a regular basis to research and collect graphics for her books on European design, which also influences her package and label designs. For example, she designed a series of bottles, jars, and boxes for Bella Cucina specialty foods—elegant, hand-packaged flavored oils, preserved lemons, biscotti, and marmellatas (marmalades). She decided to aim for a union of old-world flavor and contemporary styling, using paper-wrapped lids tied with twine that express the product's artistic food image. "Bella Cucina is a brand we've developed over the years in different forms," Fili explains. "We've been able to expand the brand and still keep the integrity of the product." So effective was the result that many customers comment that they first buy the Bella Cucina brand because of the packaging.

And because vintage type can also imply care and quality in a product, Fili designed letterforms based on turn-of-the-century cracker packaging for Late July's organic crackers, along with graphic printing imagery from that era. She's also completed other successful packaging for Tate's Bake Shop (milk carton–style containers in deep shades of green, red and purple), Vong spices (bags, bottles, and silver cans), Honolulu Coffee (green bags and cans with a stylized woman drinking coffee), Stella sauces (featuring a centered star on the label), Irving Farm Coffee (distinctive silver cans), and Bartlett Winery (white labels with a single brightly-colored fruit or flower). Her research takes her to corporations, museums, and archives in Europe, and she plans her trips around the best flea markets in France and Italy. In addition to her involvement in restaurant design and food packaging, Fili still juggles a variety of publishing projects,

(continues)

(continued)

including design collections and letterpress books. She also designs restaurant logos. "I love the challenges of designing restaurant logos," she says. "Often the name will not have been well thought out, and so it is my job to make an unpronounceable name look pronounceable, or a boring name look exciting. The downside is that in New York City, a restaurant is the number one business most likely to fail. I can design a lovely logo that will disappear after six months, to say nothing of my fee!"

When she started her own studio, she immediately learned two important lessons: "That you can never depend on any one type of work or any one client, and that you should never just sit and wait for the phone to ring with the perfect job." And so, she learned to diversify. "I learned to create my own projects," she says. "Since I was always interested in food, this was a perfect opportunity to explore the world of restaurants and food packaging.

"A supermarket can be your best classroom," she advises aspiring designers. "Look at everything you can; familiarize yourself with what is a successful design and what is not, and ask yourself why." She also recommends that you become acquainted with all of the regulations for nutritional information, ingredients, net weight, and so on—don't expect your client to know.

Design is all about love, she says. "Logos aren't cold geometric devices based on market research, but distinctive signatures that reveal the essential character of the client. It's a job for those who want elegance and for those who take pride in their products."

Pitfalls

If you work for an agency, there can be an incredible amount of pressure (both related to creativity and deadlines) to continually produce outstanding work.

Perks

If you're creative and love an artistic challenge, designing food-related packaging can be quite a kick. The job is always different and often offers unique puzzles to overcome.

Get a Jump on the Job

Take as many art, design, and graphics classes as you can in high school and college, and spend time looking at food packaging whenever you go out shopping. If you can wrangle an internship with a design company, go for it! The more experience you have in this field, the better.

FOOD SCULPTOR

OVERVIEW

A mound of butter, chocolate, or cheese may not look like much to you—but to a food sculptor, it's art waiting to happen.

Some say food sculpture has its roots in ancient Tibetan Buddhist art, where these temporary creations symbolize impermanence—a basic tenet of Buddhism. The American form of this art has more to do with sideshows and agricultural fairs, despite the fact that they're created by serious and talented artists.

The history of U.S. food sculpture began in the 1800s when frontier women molded and imprinted their own home-made butter. By the late 1800s, the idea of creating shapes out of butter caught on as a dairy promotional fixture at state fairs, although no one seems to know why. Caroline S. Brooks—the "Butter Lady" of San Francisco—was one of these first butter sculptors, earning national attention for her work in butter. J. E. Wallace appears to have been the butter sculptor of choice for early 20th-century agricultural fairs, where he often worked in large coolers holding as much as 2,700 pounds of ice as he sculpted 600-pound butter cows. Toward the end of the exhibitions, as the butter began to melt, crowds lined up to buy the softening stuff.

Today, butter sculpture remains a popular attraction at many agricultural fairs across America. The method of sculpting is quite different depending on

whether the sculptor is working in butter, chocolate, or cheese.

If you're working in butter, you'll need a cool place to create and lots of pure, unsalted butter—not margarine (it's too soft). The average sculpture requires 600 to 1,000 pounds and may take between 120 to 300 hours to complete.

For a butter sculpture, the artist first creates a metal framework (called an armature) of the creation on which to apply the butter, exactly as would happen if carving in clay. Working from large boxes of butter, the sculptor then uses a variety of tools to press and smooth the butter into shape on top of the armature. Typically, the sculptor wears gloves to improve the grip and decrease the heat applied to the butter. The ideal temperature for working with butter is 55 degrees; for

Jim Victor, food sculptor

It was a chunk of fake cheese that launched the Philadelphia sculptor into the world of food sculpting. Jim Victor had been doing sculpture portraits of celebrities for magazines and newspapers, including busts of Jimmy Carter commissioned by *New York* Magazine and of Henry Kissinger for the *New York Times*. Then he carved the likeness of a politician for the cover of the *Philadelphia Inquirer* magazine. Pictured as "The Big Cheese"—a provolone cheese hanging with a bunch of salamis—the politician was a fabrication of plaster, color, and wax, not really made of cheese at all. "But it looked like a real cheese," Victor says. The people who saw it assumed Victor was a cheese carver, and—as they say—the rest was history.

After the political cheese creation, a former student approached him about carving chocolate heads of Mickey Rooney and Ann Miller to publicize the 1000th performance of *Sugar Babies* on Broadway. At first, he was somewhat reluctant to move into the perishable sculpting profession. After all, he'd studied art in the 1960s and spent five years studying sculpture at the Pennsylvania Academy of the Fine Arts, with degrees from two different art academies. But the demand for fine-arts sculpture being what it is (or, more precisely, isn't), he realized this was another way to make money. "It's not fine art," he says, "but it's something that gives people some enjoyment."

Victor worked with chocolatier Judy Worrell to produce two busts of the stars. At the unveiling, Ann Miller bent to look at her chocolate likeness, but her foot bumped the table, which knocked off the heads. Fortunately, the chocolatier had some liquid chocolate and Victor had a Swiss army knife. Hours later, the repaired heads re-appeared, in perfect shape.

"The main thing is, there's enough work so that I can make a living doing this," he says. "And it's kind of fun. Plus I get to eat a lot of chocolate and cheese."

Chocolate portraits of Philadelphia Mayor William Green and comedian Robin Williams soon followed, and in the 1990s, Victor began creating butter sculptures for the Pennsylvania State Farm Show. This butter job led to dozens of other food sculpting jobs from Wyoming to Florida. In 2002, he was featured on the TBS TV show *Ripley's Believe it or Not*, sculpting a young woman entirely from butter. That same year he was asked to produce a 250-pound Cheesasaurus Rex out of carved Kraft cheese for the 2002 Hidalgo, Texas, Border Fest. He added "cheese carving" to his resume and never looked back.

Each food sculpture medium—butter, chocolate, or cheese—has its particular problems and advantages. "Butter is the easiest," he notes, "but temperature is the key." Once Victor builds the metal model of the sculpture, he then starts carving blocks of Grade AA unsalted butter and smoothing it over the armature.

Chocolate is totally different, Victor notes. "One of the big problems with chocolate is that for it to be done properly, it must be tempered. That makes the chocolate stronger and more stable, and it will last longer. It also gives it that sheen."

In 2004 Victor combined 200 pounds of butter and some spray-painted chocolate for the first time in a life-size sculpture of chocolate king Milton Hershey and two dairy cows for the Pennsylvania State Fair.

Cheese causes even more problems than chocolate, Victor notes, because it won't stick to itself. One of his latest cheese commissions was a replica of Terry Labonte's NASCAR racecar from 3,500 pounds of Cabot cheddar for the American Dairy Association. The car was on display at the Winston Cup race in Richmond, North Carolina, to celebrate the appearance of Labonte's machine in a "Got Milk?" campaign. "There was only about three to four inches of cheese over the wood armature," he confesses. Victor took commercial slabs of cheese and simply screwed them onto the armature, filling in the screw holes with bits of shredded cheese.

"Each one is a challenge," he says. "But I'm prepared for it. You find out what the material can do, and then you do it." The main thing, he says, is to understand the type of food you're working with. Most of the sponsoring corporations have technicians to help him with ideas, because they understand the chemistry of the food they produce.

Over the years, Victor, has produced a wide range of sculptures, including chocolate pigs, tractors, trains, and a 1957 Harley-Davidson Sportster; a Christopher Columbus from wheels of Parmesan for a New York parade; a Santa from cream cheese and mascarpone; and butter milkmaids, horses, chickens, an old milk wagon, a woman in a bikini, and all kinds of cows.

this reason, butter sculptors usually work in a refrigerated room or display case.

Chocolate sculpting is even more difficult, since it's not quite as malleable as butter and must be tempered in order to create the shiny sheen that makes chocolate look so good. Cheese sculpting is the most difficult type of food sculpture, because cheese will not stick to itself, as chocolate and butter will. To sculpt in cheese is really more like building, adding blocks of cheese on top of each other on top of a wooden base.

Pitfalls

There can be a lot of travel involved, which can become a drag. And if you don't much like cold temperatures, you probably won't care for food sculpture.

Perks

There's lots of creativity and fun involved with sculpting food—plus, you'll probably never go hungry! There's also a lot of independence and freedom, and if you've got a lot of artistic flair, you can get a lot of enjoyment from this job.

Get a Jump on the Job

Food sculptors are first and foremost artists—trained artists who are as capable sculpting in wood or marble as in more perishable materials. Get as much training as you can, as early as you can—take all the art classes available (especially in sculpture). Since sculpting in cheese, butter, or chocolate can be tricky, it might help to practice first with more traditional materials until you feel comfortable with the techniques.

FOOD SERVICE MANAGER

OVERVIEW

Whether it's at a restaurant, cafeteria, banquet hall, hotel, or resort, being a food service manager takes a steady hand and a quick mind, since you've got to juggle responsibilities in the kitchen, the dining room, and the banquet operation, while also making sure your customers are satisfied with their dining experience. As a food service manager, you'll be responsible for the daily operations of the restaurant and or other institution that prepares and serves meals and beverages to customers.

Food service managers also oversee the inventory and ordering of food, equipment, and supplies, and arrange for the routine maintenance and upkeep of the restaurant, its equipment, and facilities. Managers are generally responsible for all of the administrative and human-resource functions of running the business, including recruiting new employees and monitoring employee performance and training.

One of the most important tasks of food service managers is helping the executive chef select successful menu items. This task varies by establishment depending on what foods are in season, how often the restaurant changes its menus, and daily or weekly specials.

Managers help choose menu items ("Should we add the beef Wellington and take out the duck à l'orange? What vegetables will go with that?"). When making these decisions, you'll need to take into account how many customers you'll

AT A GLANCE

Salary Range

Average annual earnings of salaried food service managers is between $27,910 and $47,120; the lowest 10 percent earned less than $21,760, and the highest 10 percent earned more than $67,490. Those in the very top restaurants can earn six figures.

Education/Experience

A bachelor's degree in restaurant and food service management provides particularly strong preparation for this career. Many colleges and universities offer four-year programs in restaurant and hotel management or institutional food service management. For those not interested in pursuing a four-year degree, community and junior colleges, technical institutes, and other institutions offer programs in the field leading to an associate degree or other formal certification. Restaurant chains prefer to hire people with degrees in restaurant and institutional food service management, but they often hire graduates with degrees in other fields who have demonstrated interest and aptitude. Both two- and four-year programs provide instruction in subjects such as nutrition, sanitation, and food planning and preparation, as well as accounting, business law and management, and computer science. Some programs combine classroom and laboratory study with internships providing on-the-job experience. In addition, many educational institutions offer culinary programs in food preparation. Such training can lead to a career as a cook or chef and provide a foundation for advancement to an executive chef position.

Most restaurant chains and food service management companies have tough training programs for management positions including a combination of classroom and on-the-job training in all aspects of the operation of a restaurant or institutional food service facility. Areas include food preparation, nutrition, sanitation, security, company

(continues)

AT A GLANCE *(continued)*

policies and procedures, personnel management, recordkeeping, and preparation of reports. Training on use of the restaurant's computer system is increasingly important as well.

Personal Attributes

Managers should be calm, flexible, and able to work through emergencies. Self-discipline, initiative, and leadership ability are essential. Managers must be able to solve problems and concentrate on details, and they need good communication skills to deal with customers and suppliers, as well as to motivate and direct their staff. A neat and clean appearance, good health, and stamina are also important.

Requirements

The certified Foodservice Management Professional (FMP) designation is a measure of professional achievement for food service managers. Although this is not often required, voluntary certification provides recognition of professional competence, particularly for managers who acquired their skills largely on the job. The National Restaurant Association Educational Foundation awards the FMP designation to managers who achieve a qualifying score on a written examination, complete a series of courses that cover a range of food service management topics, and meet standards of work experience in the field.

Outlook

Employment of food service managers is expected to grow about as fast as the average for all occupations through 2012. In addition to job openings because of new businesses, the need to replace managers who transfer to other occupations or stop working will create lots of vacancies. Applicants with a bachelor's or an associate degree in restaurant and institutional food service management should have the best job opportunities, but a willingness to relocate often is essential in landing a job.

be getting and how popular dishes like this were in the past. Other issues when planning a menu include whether there was any unserved food left over from prior meals that shouldn't be wasted, the need for variety, and the seasonal availability of foods. Managers or executive chefs analyze the recipes of the dishes to determine food, labor, and overhead costs and to assign prices to various dishes. Menus must be developed far enough in advance that supplies can be ordered and received in time.

Managers also estimate food needs, place orders with distributors, and schedule the delivery of fresh food and supplies. They plan for routine services or deliveries, such as linen services or the heavy cleaning of dining rooms or kitchen equipment, to occur during slow times or when the dining room is closed. Managers also take care of equipment maintenance and repairs, and coordinate services such as waste removal and pest control. You'll also need to be on hand to receive deliveries and check the contents against order records, inspect the quality of fresh meats, poultry, fish, fruits, vegetables, and baked goods to ensure that expectations are met. Then you'll need to meet with representatives from restaurant supply companies and place orders to replenish stocks of tableware, linens, paper products, cleaning supplies, cooking utensils, and furniture and fixtures.

Pitfalls

If your head is swimming after reading all of the responsibilities that go into the job of food service manager, you'll understand what the pitfalls of this career can be. Food service managers are among the first to arrive in the morning and the last to leave

Ray Hottenstein, restaurant owner and manager

In Ray Hottenstein's opinion, the best food service managers are a bit like puppeteers, overseeing every aspect of the restaurant. "You've got to be able to deal with the plumber at the same time as the chef, the energy company, and the advertising agency, all while trying to develop a relationship with 40,000 friends," he laughs.

Hottenstein should know. As food service manager and owner of the Olde Greenfield Inn in Lancaster, Pennsylvania, he's spent 14 years juggling those kinds of responsibilities, and he'll be the first to tell you that if you want to succeed as a food service manager, you've got to be willing to dedicate a lot of hours to the job. "You can't be in this business and not love what you do," he says. "Some people can get away with being at a restaurant less than others. Me, I tend to be the type of person who thinks I should be here all the time. I have friends of mine who can walk away for a day or two at a time, but for me—if I take three days off, people will say: 'I heard you were on vacation!'"

Despite being on the job every single day, Hottenstein loves what he does and accepts the fact that to be successful, he has to work hard. "I like the idea of being self-employed," he says. "I've worked for other folks and with other folks throughout my life, and I know that in this kind of business, if you're going to work as hard as you have to do to be successful, you might as well be successful at something you love."

Hottenstein started out as a part-time bartender, eventually moving on to full-time bartending, and then learned other aspects of the restaurant business. He spent quite a bit of time working on his kitchen skills. "I would never want to assume the title of 'chef,'" Hottenstein says, "but I would encourage any food service professional who is not kitchen oriented to get some experience there. If you're a food service manager, you've got to know if the chef is making the sauce the way you want it." In fact, this is so important that Hottenstein recommends food service managers take cooking classes to learn the basic principles.

"The money is made and the money is lost in the kitchen," he explains. "That's the heart of the operation, and that's why a good food service manager must know something about what happens in the kitchen."

It didn't use to be so important for food service managers to have a formal education in the business, but these days Hottenstein thinks a solid understanding of business is a must. "You need to understand Excel, and be able to read computer spreadsheets. You've got to be able to figure out what stuff costs 24 hours a day." If a restaurant sells a beef dish that includes a side vegetable and a salad, the food service manager must know what every ingredient costs and how it affects the overall price of the meal. "If you include bread, butter, and salad with a beef dish," Hottenstein says, "maybe your beef hasn't increased in price, but your base for the premium peppercorn house dressing increased 65 cents along with the price of Bibb lettuce. All of a sudden, the cost of the salad has doubled." Produce prices typically change dramatically because of cost in gas to transport it, and because of the impact that weather has on crops.

at night. Long hours—that's 12 to 15 hours a day, 50 hours or more a week, often for seven days a week—are common.

Managers also should be able to fill in for absent workers on short notice. If your maitre d' didn't show up or your

In fact, he says that most people don't realize that the average restaurant only earns a 5 percent profit. "When they see you smiling and laughing and having a great time out front—because that's part of your job—and the cash is coming in and people are swiping credit cards, customers don't realize that that $75 check for two people turns into a $3.50 net profit for the restaurant. And that's only if someone didn't drop a glass."

To be a successful food service manager, in addition to working hard and learning kitchen skills, Hottenstein also recommends that you join the local restaurant association. As president of the Pennsylvania Restaurant Association, Hottenstein has been involved in the association at the local and state level for years. "I believe all food service professionals should be part of that type of association," he explains. "Every time I sit down with a bunch of guys or girls at the restaurant association, I learn something. Maybe you've had a problem for six years, and all of a sudden when you meet with other food professionals, someone will say: 'Here's how to deal with it.' You may learn from people who are half your age. They've looked at a problem altogether from a different point of view."

Still, to some extent—no matter how good the food service manager is—the restaurant business is always at the mercy of outside influences. "We had our first down quarter in 14 years last year," he says. "You get to the point where you're comfortable with what you're doing, you have a great staff, and all of a sudden something happens that you can't control." In the past year he's seen a big drop in clientele because of social and political setbacks. "It's tough to have good time when 130,000 of your brightest young people are in harm's way in Iraq," he says. The war, along with the devastating hurricanes and floods in this country, has hurt the restaurant industry, Hottenstein says. "You have to feel good to want to go out," he says. "This is very much an emotional business. And the general increase in gas prices has taken a huge toll out of people's pockets, too. If you're spending $60 or $80 more a month for gas—why, that's a lot of money, and that's what you might have spent at the Greenfield Inn."

Hottenstein says he used to discourage young people from getting into the business, because he thought it was such a tough way to earn a living. "But now, there are so many avenues to make it a success," he says, "and so many great people looking for young people to work in their restaurants." There's still a place for success as a food service manager, as long as you have a solid work ethic, he believes. "You must come in early and stay late," he advises. "If you just come to work when you're supposed to be there, that's not good enough. If you're the night manager and you're supposed to be there at 4 p.m., you'd better be there by 3, because that's what an owner is looking for—that extra push. That guy who takes the extra step, she or he's burning the midnight oil—that's who will be successful. It's a tough racket, but a very exciting racket."

bartender called in sick, you're the one who's probably got to don the tie or the apron and fill in. This adds up to mega-pressure, which is worsened by needing to simultaneously coordinate a wide range of activities. When problems occur, it's the manager's responsibility to resolve them with minimal disruption to customers. Stove on fire in the kitchen? Plate of lobsters just slid onto the floor in the prep room? You can't let on in the front of the house that anything is amiss. The job can be hectic, and dealing with irate customers or uncooperative employees can be stressful.

Perks

Oddly enough, this kind of stress actually appeals to some people, and these are the ones who gravitate to this kind of job. Juggling lots of different responsibilities seamlessly can be a real adrenaline boost to some individuals, who thrive on the challenge. If you love people and the food business, this job gives you the responsibility to do it all. Those who rise to the very top of the profession can also expect to be well paid for their stress.

Get a Jump on the Job

The best way to get an idea of what the restaurant business is really like is to get a job there—even in high school, you can work as a bus person or in some type of kitchen job, washing glasses or preparing salads. A few restaurants that don't serve alcohol may be willing to hire wait staff as young as 16, although 18 may be more typical. Study hard and think about majoring in some food or hotel-related area in college, and during college, get jobs in lots of different restaurants and food establishments to learn more about the business. Even as a kitchen helper or waitperson, you'll get a very good idea of the kind of stress involved and whether this might be something you'd like to do.

FOOD STYLIST

OVERVIEW

Great-looking food doesn't just happen. It takes a lot of ability and expertise to make a sandwich or other food look just the way it's supposed to for a photo in a magazine or cookbook, or on a TV show, movie, or commercial. Although it might not seem like a big deal, food styling is very important. After all, who's going to want to take time to prepare, or spend money to buy a sandwich that doesn't look good? You can bet that the food you see in pictures or on TV has been carefully styled to make it look appealing and appetizing.

Have you ever seen a magazine photo of a juicy steak that makes your mouth water just by looking at it? Those effects are the results of a food stylist, who does everything necessary to get food ready to be photographed or filmed. This might include conferring with photographers, clients, producers, advertising representatives, or others to find out exactly what is expected and required. Once you have a thorough understanding of what the job entails, you need to get the food, equipment, and anything else you'll need to the location of the shoot. The food must be prepared and then styled to look its best.

Food stylists work in varied settings and under many different circumstances. One day might be spent outside, arranging for a photograph of picnic foods to appear in a cookbook or magazine. The next day the stylist could be in an advertising studio preparing food for a TV commercial. Food stylists also prepare and style foods for movies and TV shows.

Because life is full of surprises, a food stylist must always be prepared to deal with the unexpected. A sudden gust of wind, for instance, can wreak havoc with a carefully arranged picnic setting. A delayed photo shoot can result in wilted produce and worse, and require that the food be re-prepared and styled.

Experienced food stylists have many tricks and use a wide range of equipment—some of which you wouldn't expect to be associated with food. In addition to the usual spatulas, measuring cups, hot pads, knives, and so forth, a food stylist might rely on cotton swabs to clean the edges of plates and bowls, tweezers to make sure a small piece of food or garnish is placed exactly where it needs to be, and spray bottles to keep foods such as lettuce misted and fresh-looking.

Food styling can be unpredictable, and often requires long hours and irregular schedules. Many food stylists work on a freelance basis, and some rely on second jobs to supplement their incomes, especially when they are just breaking into the field.

In addition to culinary skills and a knowledge of photography, if you'll be working on a freelance basis you'll also need some business know-how in order to be successful as a food stylist. You'll need to be willing and able to promote yourself to prospective clients; keep track of billing, scheduling, and expenses; and attend to other necessary matters.

In addition to culinary training, the best way to learn the job of styling food is to work with an experienced stylist as an assistant. You might be able to locate a stylist through one of the associations listed in Appendix A.

Pitfalls

Competition for food styling jobs is keen, although job availability may vary from region to region. It requires time to acquire a reputation in food styling, meaning that you might need to work for low wages for several years until you've established yourself.

Perks

Food styling allows you to be creative, and no two jobs are ever the same. There's plenty of variation involved with food styling jobs, so a high-energy, artistic person can continue to be challenged and inspired. Once you are established as an experienced food stylist, you may have opportunities to instruct others.

Get a Jump on the Job

Check out the Internet for Web sites relating to food styling. You can find interviews with food stylists, and there are even names of food stylists who are willing to be contacted with questions. Study photographs of foods and try to get a sense of why the food is presented in a particular manner. Style the food that's prepared and served in your home.

Brian Preston-Campbell, food stylist

Brian Preston-Campbell's client list includes a who's who of restaurants; food, beverage, and cookware manufacturers; magazines and other publications; and food councils. He also has worked for Walt Disney World, the Food Network, and the New York Sports Club. Preston-Campbell, you might say, is well connected within the food styling business.

He did not, however, train in food styling. In fact, he's never taken any formal classes in food styling, although they are offered at culinary schools. Preston-Campbell's training is in culinary arts, and he spent 11 years cooking in restaurants. "That was fine at first," he says. "But, after doing basically the same task at several different restaurants over the course of those 11 years, I knew I needed to make a change."

Preston-Campbell had heard about food styling from a colleague who was working part time as a food stylist's assistant, and thought it sounded interesting. He continued the restaurant work as he explored the possibility of becoming a food stylist. After a time, he was ready to make the move.

"The transition from chef to food stylist did take some time," Preston-Campbell says. "It was about three years before I was able to work full time in food styling. Fortunately, business has gradually increased every year."

Getting started in food styling takes time because you need to develop media contacts and establish a portfolio with which to attract clients. Once he had both a portfolio and a client list, Preston-Campbell got busy. Eventually, he hired some assistants and has become well known as a stylist. While he still looks for work, clients will also contact him about upcoming jobs.

He styles just about anything the client asks for, from a dripping tower of multi-colored fruit Popsicles to a perfectly browned, stuffed turkey on a plate, to a cherry-garnished apple martini. The trick, he says, is to make the food for every job look its best and able to remain looking its best until the photography has been completed.

Clients occasionally deliver to Preston-Campbell the products that they want to have styled for photography. More often than not, however, he and his assistants shop for, buy, and prepare all the necessary foods.

"On occasion, the product to be featured is delivered to us," Preston-Campbell says. "More frequently, we are required to seek out hard-to-find items and out-of-season produce in order to complete the shots."

What you see in a food photograph is not always what it seems, Preston-Campbell revealed. The "ice" in drinks usually is made from glass or acrylic to prevent melting under hot camera lights. The beads of moisture on the outside of the glass usually are a mixture of water and glycerin, which doesn't evaporate as quickly as plain water would. A nicely browned chicken appears to be cooked on the outside, but may be practically raw inside. To save time, and prevent the chicken skin from drying out and wrinkling during a long cooking time, the chicken might be cooked very quickly in a hot oven, and then brushed with a browning agent to make it appear golden brown and crispy.

The grill marks on a juicy-looking steak might have been applied with a hot skewer rather than having been acquired on a grill. This allows the stylist to apply the lines in a more uniform and attractive fashion, Preston-Campbell says.

(continues)

(continued)

He is relieved, however, that the trend of using fake or inedible foods that was popular several years ago has been reversed. "There still are some tricks that are sometimes necessary, but usually I am expected to cook real food," he says.

Many of Preston-Campbell's assignments as of late have shifted from food to beverage styling, an area that he enjoys. "It's a nice change from cooked food," he says. "I've made everything from smoothies, to a beer with a perfect head, to a cold-looking bottle of Coke. The challenge is to create the illusion of a cold, refreshing beverage that will look good for the time required by the photographer to set the lighting and assess the shot."

While some food stylists have assistants who do most of the actual food preparation, Preston-Campbell says it's important to have a good culinary background. Some food stylists he knows were trained in art or film production, while others have home economics degrees. Still, he feels, it's important to have some formal culinary training and get some experience working with accomplished chefs in respected restaurants.

The best thing about being a food stylist, Preston-Campbell says, is that every day is different from the last.

"I am definitely not the type of person who would enjoy going to the same place, performing the same tasks repetitively, and interacting with the same people every day," he says. "As it is, in a given week I could be working with three or four photographers in just about any location in the New York City area, for all different types of clients and with all different kinds of food to be styled."

The downside of styling food, according to Preston-Campbell, is that there almost inevitably will be some flops. "It's very rare, but every now and then the food does not photograph the way I had planned, or the client requests something that's virtually impossible, or the herbs arrive in a sorry state."

Still, he says, even when there are problems, he wouldn't trade his job for another. He simply chalks the problem up to experience and moves on. "Small factors can sometimes get in the way of the creative process and make my job difficult," Preston-Campbell says. "The only solution is to wade through it, and remember that when the job is done, I'll be moving along to the next project."

GOURMET FOOD BUSINESS OWNER

OVERVIEW

It begins with a dream, a flair for cooking or baking, a yen for independence, and a hunger for creative freedom. But no matter how much talented chefs, bakers, and foodies want that dream to become a reality, they can't rely only on their expertise in cooking.

To be a successful gourmet food business owner, you also need to develop business and financial skills as well as a mean enchilada, a yummy cookie recipe, or a tasty marinade. You might make the best babka this side of Belarus, but if you can't write a business plan, set up a marketing scheme, and secure the financing, you'll just be another entrepreneur with a dream.

If you do have the marketing and financial smarts—plus a good product—and you get your business up and running, don't expect to sit back, tend the cash register, and watch the money rolling in. You'll also need to spend a lot of time marketing and promoting your gourmet food products and building a steady clientele. If you sell your product from a storefront, you'll need to figure out how to design your signs and your building and how to arrange your merchandise to increase sales. You'll need to constantly fine-tune your business to keep growing and boost the bottom line. You'll also need to consider whether to offer a Web

site and whether to sell your products online. Maintaining online sales means you'll need to constantly update your Web site to attract new and repeat business.

Mike Lampros, co-owner of Gunther's Gourmet Groceries

When Mike Lampros first started out at culinary school, he had no idea that one day he'd own his own gourmet food products company. After graduating from the University of Richmond and the Culinary Institute of America and getting his executive chef certification, Lampros landed a job as executive chef for the Reynolds Metals Company. That's when he started experimenting with making his own salsas and marinades.

He was particularly proud of his orange balsamic vinaigrette marinade. When a food company advertised a national recipe contest, he was tempted to send in his brainchild—until he consulted with his older brother Nick, a lawyer, pointed out that if Mike submitted the recipe to the contest, he'd lose all rights to his creation. Nick advised Mike to sell the product himself.

That's exactly what he did. He fine-tuned his recipe and came up with a name for the company—Gunther's Gourmet. Yet with a great recipe and a catchy company name, it still took him almost two years to launch the company. "I was still a chef, working every day," he explains. "If you go into the culinary field, you have to realize that you work when other people want to have fun—Mother's Day, Easter, Christmas, New Years' Day, weekends—you're always in the kitchen. You get weird days off and you work all the time—a short day is 10 hours. You have to be dedicated."

He consulted with three different graphic design firms to come up with a unique logo for his budding food products company. "Our label is simple and elegant," he says. "That's the first thing that sells people on a product—the look of the label. But the product itself is what causes people to come back and buy again."

Still working full time as a chef, he spent all his spare time working out the details: UPC codes, health regulations, USDA approval, sanitary codes, health inspections, FDA label rules—and finding a bottler to produce his all-natural recipe.

"It's not like making things in your kitchen," he says. The heat during pasteurization changes the flavor, so he had to tinker with the recipe in the beginning so that he ended up with the flavor he was looking for after the pasteurization process. "A lot of people produce food out of their own house, in small batches," he says. "We wanted to bottle professionally. I think a lot of people get weirded out at the thought of buying food prepared in somebody's kitchen."

Finally, the marinade was bottled, labeled, and ready to go. On his days off from the restaurant, he'd drive around the county, trying to entice stores to carry his product. "You think you're special with one flavor," he says, "but there's a whole bunch of you out there." Stores were reluctant to buy a product from a one-product company. "I'd do research, drive around, and hit small stores in nearby towns," he recalls. Eventually, he quit his full-time job as executive chef to pitch his product during the day, working nights and weekends at a friend's restaurant. "If a store bought a case of marinade, when they had a wine tasting I'd be there handing out the product. Then I'd move to the next city, and the next, while keeping up with all the stores I already had. Good customer service is important. I'd talk to people, do some samplings.

Eventually he branched out, using the finest ingredients he could find to develop a uniquely flavored line of marinades, vinaigrettes, and salsas that are all-natural and healthy, ending up with a 10-flavor lineup.

His advice to young chef wanna-bes? Get an education. Go to college first, and then get a four-year degree from a culinary school, he says. "These days, it's a lot harder to get into culinary school and stay in," he says. "The field isn't just accepting anybody anymore." The benefit of a four-year culinary program over a two-year stint is that the in-depth four year program will teach you not just how to cook, but how to handle the business end of the food business. That will ultimately make you much more valuable as a chef when you graduate. "To be a chef you have to run a business," he says. "It's not just about cooking. You wear a lot of hats."

Few people graduate from culinary school and jump right into their own food products business. It takes time to build up the experience. "The school of hard knocks is the best teacher around," he says. "You have to get in there, swallow your pride, be the low man on the totem pole, keep your mouth shut, and in due time you'll get your own kitchen and get to do things your way. You need to open your mind, because every chef teaches something different. The more you listen, the more options you'll have when you run your own restaurant or your own business. You've got to put your ego in your back pocket."

He loves the freedom that comes from running his own gourmet food products company. "I don't have to answer to anybody else," he says. "With this company, you're putting your name and reputation on the line. Hopefully you have a good product that lives up to the name."

The most difficult part was getting started. "It's hard and depressing, when you only have one flavor, to go out every day and only sell one carton," he says. "And then you have to put a smiley face on and you have to go to work at a friend's restaurant.

"Basically we've made it by word of mouth. In four years we've gone from zero stores to being carried in stores around the country. We've been really fortunate, and my friends all help. People get excited and want to help out." Publicity also helps—articles about the company have appeared in *Southern Living* and *Health* magazine, and there's been lots of good local press.

Although the company is now in negotiations with chain stores to carry their product, Mike says he still takes personal care of his original clients. "I feel a good deal of loyalty to them," he says. "But to make this company viable we need to become more appealing to store chains, not just one store around the corner, although we love to sell to them too."

The company also does a brisk business online (http://www.gunthersgourmet.com), shipping to 40 states and abroad. "Being in *Southern Living* really bumped up our sales," he says. "And a lot of families with kids in the military send our products to their kids abroad."

Once Gunther's Gourmet products are picked up by some larger chain stores, Mike plans to bring out a few more flavors. It may seem like a fun, creative, romantic way to make a living, but Mike makes it clear that it's a tough business. "Every day you've got to get out there, every single day." And the competition is fierce. You'll be competing with big companies that can get a product in the jar for 99 cents. "The quality isn't quite there, but the consumer says: 'Do I want to buy this at $3.59, or that one for 99 cents?'"

Today, Gunther's Gourmet Groceries, based in Richmond, Virginia, offers a variety of vinaigrette marinades (including lemon-oregano, roasted garlic/sun-dried tomato, and orange-balsamic) and a range of salsas (from hearty black/white bean to tropical lime/mango).

"Nobody does it better than you do, because it's your name on the line," he says. "You're the one who cares the most about it."

Pitfalls

When it comes to opening up your own business, no matter how much you love the products, the pitfalls are many! Running a gourmet food business sounds romantic and fun, but you'll need solid business and financial skills to run your own business.

Perks

If you love cooking or food, and you have developed some great recipes, it just makes sense to want to try to sell your product to others—and if you're successful, what could be more fun?

Get a Jump on the Job

If there's a gourmet food store in your future, you could start right now in working up recipes and trying out different variations on your family and friends. Consider working part time after school or in the summers at a gourmet food store, a bakery, or restaurant. Spend time thinking about why successful gourmet shops in your neighborhood are successful—is it location? Product? Value? Or all three? In school, take business courses and think about whether you want to attend culinary school.

ICE CREAM TASTE TESTER

OVERVIEW

What could be more fun than going to work to taste endless varieties of ice cream? Being a taste tester is probably the stuff of every kid's dreams, with visions of endless supplies of Rocky Road and Jamocha Almond Fudge.

For a taste tester, the job is just that—but much, much more. Being a taste tester for an ice cream company means that you're checking each carton to make sure the ice cream is up to snuff, containing the right ingredients in the right amounts so the public won't be disappointed. To that end, an ice cream taste tester tastes and approves or rejects every flavor produced by an ice cream company, sampling a number of cartons from each run on a daily basis (usually, a taster samples from the beginning, middle, and end of each flavor batch made). This ensures the consistent quality of the finished product to the consumer. Tasters also may be involved in coming up with new ice cream flavors in some food companies.

The ice cream taster tastes ice cream at about 10 to 12 degrees F, to maximize all the flavor in the container—warming up the ice cream a bit also helps to avoid numbing the taste buds. And nothing is more important to a taste tester than those 9,000 taste buds, each with 10 to 15 receptacles sending messages of "bitter, sweet, salty, or sour" to the brain. When sampling ice cream, the main focus of the taste buds is to decipher the quality

top notes and balance of the fresh cream, sweeteners, and natural flavors.

Because the it's important to be able to keep those taste buds in tip-top shape so as to be able to distinguish the subtleties of ice cream, taste testers typically protect their taste buds by avoiding spicy foods, caffeine, pepper, alcohol, and smoking—and even avoid strong smells.

Typically, once a taster has tasted and spat out the sample, he or she will then cut the carton in half lengthwise to check the distribution of the added ingredients.

John Harrison, ice cream taste tester

As the official taster for Oakland, California–based Dreyer's and Edy's Grand ice creams, John Harrison gets paid to taste ice cream every day. In fact, his talented taste buds are so important to Edy's that they're insured for $1 million! Over the years, Harrison taste buds have sampled more than 180 million gallons of ice cream.

"It's a fun position," Harrison says. "Even though Dryers/Edy's is paying me, I really represent the industry. I was on TV in Syracuse giving statistics, explaining about how ice cream came about, providing information for the industry. Really, I've become an industry spokesman. And that's been fun, it's not an infomercial—it's just industry information. I'm unique because of my background and knowing ice cream." In fact, Harrison doesn't just know ice cream—he loves it, just as his father, his father's father, and his grandfather's father have done. In 1880, Harrison's great-grandfather owned two ice cream parlors in turn-of-the-century New York City; his grandfather had the first dairy co-op in Tennessee, and his father owned a dairy ingredients company in Atlanta. In addition, his Uncle Tom Harrison owned an ice cream factory in Memphis. "That's where I grew up," he recalls, "eating my way through the summer. I learned how to formulate ice cream, the nuances of fresh cream, milk, sugars, and ingredients like raspberry, blueberry, and caramel. Having grown up with ice cream and talking about it with my father, it's just second nature." In fact, his ice cream roots are so firmly planted that he claims: "My blood runs 16 percent butterfat."

His tasting day begins at 7:30 a.m., when his 9,000 taste buds are at their peak. Wielding a gold spoon (it doesn't leave an aftertaste, as wood or plastic does) he starts tasting first thing in morning, avoiding drinking any morning coffee. "Caffeine will clog the taste buds," he explains. In fact, taste buds are so delicate, they last just about 12 days. This means they're rejuvenated continually—every 12 days, you've got a brand new set. Every morning, before he begins his tasting chores, Harrison sips tea to prepare his palate.

Although sweet tastes are sensed on the tongue, "you get the top notes [of ice cream flavor] from the nose and the olfactory nerve in the forehead," Harrison says. "That's why when you get a cold or the flu, you don't like to eat. You don't get the flavor of food when you're sick, because right next to the olfactory nerve is the sinus nerve. When you get a cold or flu, that nerve swells and blocks the olfactory." (The olfactory nerve is also the source of that "ice cream headache" you get when you eat something very cold. To alleviate that stabbing pain, Harrison says, touch your tongue to the roof of your mouth. It will warm up the olfactory nerve and your headache will disappear.)

Each day, the plant makes 20 flavors, he explains—and he tastes each flavor three times a day. As he tastes, Harrison checks to see if the ice cream looks appetizing. "Flavor, balance, body, and texture—all must be equal for you to have a good eating experience. I'm looking for rich and creamy." That's 60 packages he must taste. "It's just like a wine tasting," he says. "I taste and spit. I begin with vanilla, and then I work my way up to the heavier Bordeaux of ice cream—black walnut, mint chocolate chip."

Still, Harrison confesses that he doesn't like spitting that good ice cream away, but he knows the importance of making sure each carton is exactly right. "I know companies that went bankrupt because they weren't taste tasting ice cream before it went out to the public," he says. One company, Harrison recalls, accidentally used some tainted vanilla in their product. "They thought they were using vanilla, but it was something weird—some chemical," Harrison notes. After the dust from the lawsuits cleared, the company went bankrupt. So important is quality control that Edy's gives Harrison free rein. "Something isn't right, they tell me: 'You pull the plug.'" In 2004, he says, the company donated a half million gallons of butter pecan ice cream to food banks, because there were too many pecans in those cartons. "Too much is just as wrong as not enough," he explains. "You can't be inconsistent." Big companies that have gone out of business "took their eye off the ball, they compromised," he says. "We'll be gone if we take our eyes off the ball." As a result, he's also sent around the country to check the product in the grocery stores. Unlike most other companies, Edy's delivers its own ice cream in its own trucks, because it's fussy about keeping the temperature just right. "The number one issue with ice cream is temperature," Harrison says. "If it warms up and then refreezes, it will destroy the taste. That's why we try to handle the ice cream, and we deliver every package to every store ourselves." But once it gets to the grocery store, anything could happen—sluggish or broken freezers, loss of electricity, doors left open—which is why Harrison travels around the country doing spot-tastes at various grocery stores. He also trains tasters at the company' plants on the new flavors and products.

He loves his job, but he's not so crazy about the travel—which he does for six months of the year, hitting about 50 major markets a year. In addition to tasting, he spends quite a lot of time talking about ice cream.

Being a fourth generation ice cream expert, Harrison knows the history, the trivia, and the background of ice cream. "It's a changing industry," he says. "When I started with Edy's 23 years ago, we had 16 flavors, and only one style: classic ice cream. Today we have at least 10 different styles: classic, light, slow churned, homemade, frozen yogurt, sherbet, sorbet, no sugar added … and we have 200 flavors." Edy's also offers "limited edition" flavors based on things such as apple pie, pumpkin, eggnog, and Girl Scout cookies.

Years ago, Harrison himself developed new flavors, including Cookies 'N Cream. He also influenced the creation of New York Blueberry Cheesecake, Peaches 'N Cream, and Malt Ball 'N Fudge. He received the Master Taster of the Year award in 1997 from the American Tasting Institute. At 63, Harrison's taste buds are still in their prime.

If you're thinking about becoming an ice cream taste tester, the most important thing is to get either a dairy science or food science degree. "You'll learn about ice cream from a nose standpoint," he says, "the appearance, and the texture. Whether something is right or wrong. I know in seconds."

For anyone out there interested in his job, Harrison recommends: "Sample, sample, sample! It's great to have aspirations, dream, visions," he says. "Everybody has said for decades I've got the best Willy Wonka job in America." But someday, Harrison admits, "I'm gonna have to hang up the bow tie and gold spoon." Someone else will have to step into his place. Will it be a fifth generation Harrison? Not likely, he says; none of his five children seem interested in the job. "But, I've got three wonderful grandsons. It may skip a generation!

"We're not through with our star flavors. There are still others on the horizon and the next generation is going to be those creative people who bring that out."

For example, in a carton of butter pecan, the pecans should be evenly swirled and distributed throughout the container. Too few or too many pecans, and the carton is rejected. Why would consumers have a have a problem with too many pecans? Because consistency is the watchword of any food company. If someone gets lots of pecans one week, and the correct amount the next—which means, a lot less than the week before—he or she won't be happy. So the goal is to have the exact amount of pecans in every single batch of ice cream.

Pitfalls

You don't really get to eat all that ice cream—just like a wine taster, the ice cream taster puts the ice cream in the mouth, swirls it around, and then has to spit it back out. And top taste testers in a company typically must travel to other plants to train testers there, which can get to be a bit of a drag.

Perks

If you love ice cream—and who doesn't? —this can be a dream job. You can be involved in the creative development of new ice cream flavors, in addition to making sure the ice cream your company produces is up to snuff. Some companies also use their taster as a publicity generator, sending the taster around the country on goodwill jaunts.

Get a Jump on the Job

If you're interested in taste testing for the ice cream business, it helps to have lots of experience—so grab a spoon! Aim for getting a summer job at an ice cream shop, store, or production factory.

ICE SCULPTOR

OVERVIEW

While some artists spend their entire careers creating fine works of art to last into the ages, ice sculptors know that nothing they make is permanent. In fact, the average ice sculpture only lasts between six and eight hours—and that's when it's kept at room temperature and not exposed to wind or sunlight.

Sculpting creations out of ice began more than 200 years ago, when French chefs created functional food holders to keep items cold during elaborate buffets for which the French were renowned. At the turn of the 18th century, Russians joined in perfecting this art form, which was next popularized by Japanese chefs in the mid-20th century. Currently considered masters of this art form, Japanese ice sculptors think of this job as a full-time profession, carving wood in the summer and ice in the winter.

Most ice sculptors enter the field from culinary or art backgrounds, so ice-sculpting training is offered as part of some culinary programs. Artists who move into ice sculpting usually have experience in sculpting with other media, and for one reason or another decide they'd prefer to work with ice instead.

However they arrived in the profession, carving artwork out of ice is rarely boring. Ice sculptors might one day find themselves carving tiny glasses or specialized ice cubes, and the next day they'll be hard at work carving a full-sized ice car or a celebrity look-alike figure. Ice sculptors have created chilly versions of Hogwarts (Harry Potter's school); the Nina, Pinta, and Santa Maria;

AT A GLANCE

Salary Range

Earnings vary tremendously, based on how well the sculptor is known, the location in which he or she works, and the type of clients. The median salary of an ice sculptor is $35,260, with the lowest 10 percent earning less than $16,900, and the top 10 percent making more than $73,560. Many ice sculptors work on a freelance basis. A top-rate, in-demand ice sculptor can make hundreds of thousands of dollars a year.

Education/Experience

Most ice sculptors come from either an art or a culinary background, so training or a degree in a related field, such as culinary arts or fine arts, is helpful. Some ice sculptors also offer lessons to those who wish to learn the trade.

Personal Attributes

Ice sculptors must be artistically inclined, able to visualize a concept and see it through to a finished product. Carving ice involves a variety of hand and power tools that require strength and agility to use. Also, large ice sculptures can only be produced from large blocks of ice, which are heavy to move around. People skills come in handy when it's time to deal with customers in arranging for and delivering work.

Requirements

You'll need a portfolio of your work in order to show prospective customers what you can do. Also, if you'll be working for yourself, you'll need business skills in order to keep track of orders and billing.

Outlook

Jobs in many sectors of the hospitality and food service industry, including ice sculpting, are expected to increase by between 10 and 20 percent through the year 2012. That job growth is considered to be average, according to government statistics.

giant fish; life-size sports and entertainment celebrities; giant baskets; crystal balls; plates; cutlery; glasses; corporate logos; and flower vases. In fact, nearly anything a customer can envision and is willing to pay for can be created from a block of ice.

Ice sculptors create objects ranging from two inches high to larger-than-life, which are then used for decorations at events ranging from weddings or birthday parties to corporate functions and outdoor carnivals and festivals.

While some ice sculptors work only with hand tools, others find that a chain saw is absolutely necessary to the craft. (Remember that sculptors work with blocks of ice that weigh 200 or 300 pounds or more.) Power tools are useful in ice carving because they allow the sculptor to work faster and finish the job before the ice gets too soft to work with effectively. The average amount of time an ice sculptor spends on a project is between two and three hours, and ice sculptors who carve ice competitively learn to work even faster.

So where does all that ice come from? Some ice sculptors buy blocks of ice, while others make their own. Ice for carving must be made in a special way to control the number of bubbles in the water and create the clearest ice possible. A block of ice that has a cloudy or white center is less valuable than one that is crystal clear.

Some ice sculptors work for large food service companies, hotels, or restaurants, but many are self-employed or work for an established ice sculptor who has more work than he or she can handle. Some ice sculptors have their own studios, complete with freezers and ice-making equipment. Ice sculptures can be made indoors or outside when the temperature is cold enough. Many artists work in freezers, but some prefer to work in cold-but-not-freezing areas because the ice is not as

brittle and prone to breaking as it is when it's below 32 degrees. Most ice sculptors wear protective clothing and gloves to protect themselves from the cold. When an ice sculpture is completed, it can be stored in a freezer until it's ready for delivery.

Competitive ice carving is often performed outdoors during festivals and carnivals in cold climates. These events can be very popular, drawing thousands of people and resulting in great publicity for the sculptors. Ice sculpting has even been added to the Winter Olympic games as a cultural competition.

Pitfalls

Regardless of how warmly you dress, working with huge blocks of ice for extended periods of time is a cold venture. Moreover, moving and cutting large pieces of ice is hard work. If you're the sort of person who can't bear to let go of anything you've ever made, you might want to look at another type of sculpture as a career.

Perks

Sculpting large blocks of ice into intricate crystal figures is extremely creative work that allows the artist to visualize a concept and bring it to life. Many ice sculptors feel that their work is more special and valuable because it doesn't last. Ice sculptors who carve competitively during outdoor carnivals and festivals find plenty of camaraderie and lasting friendships from joining in competitive teams.

Get a Jump on the Job

Find an ice sculptor in your area who offers lessons. You can find a list of sculptors and their locations on the National Ice Carving Association Web site. If you live in an area where ice carving competitions are held, attend the events and try to talk to some of the carvers when they're not busy.

Michael Campe, ice sculptor

Former chef Michael Campe made a name for himself after more than 20 years of cooking for fine restaurants, country clubs, and hotels. He's also an artist who's becoming increasingly noticed for his ice carvings, which range from simple to intricate.

Campe began dabbling in ice carving when he was a chef, and found that he very much enjoyed the process. Cooking, on the other hand, required long and irregular hours, leaving little time to carve ice. When Campe had an opportunity a few years back to give up restaurant work and take a job teaching cooking at a Denver culinary school, he decided to give it a go. Working regular teaching hours—7 a.m. to 3 p.m. five days a week—gave Campe more time for carving ice. As word of his availability got around, the calls started pouring in. "So now I have an ice carving business that I work at several nights a week," Campe says.

His clients range from soon-to-be brides to businesses looking for something special for a corporate meeting or holiday employee party. He gets calls from meeting planners, wedding planners, liquor companies, hotels, and individuals. "The clientele for ice carving includes just about everybody," Campe says.

Although customers request ice carvings all year, the busiest times are typically in the spring and early summer, and during the winter holiday season. Mother's Day and weddings create a large demand for carvings in May and June, while holiday parties—many of them corporate— make for busy Novembers and Decembers. Campe recently had a very hectic Mother's Day, completing 24 carvings for hotels presenting holiday buffets. He could have taken more jobs, he says, but he prefers to pick and choose the ones he wants, and to pass the rest along to other ice sculptors who are looking for more work.

"I really enjoy the work, don't get me wrong," Campe says. "But I don't want it to get to be drudgery because I always have too much to do."

Campe can, and has, carved just about any sort of ice sculpture his clients have requested. He once was hired to carve a 10-foot-high Cinderella carriage for a wedding, along with "glass" slippers for every table. Swans, kissing doves, flower vases, and intertwined hearts are popular ice sculptures for weddings. Corporate tastes lean more toward company logos, full-size ice bars, mountains with waterfalls, and shot glasses.

Basically, Campe says, he can carve anything a customer wants. "I just did one for a wedding where the bride and groom were both really into fishing," he says. "I carved two fish holding up a heart for them."

Campe's son has joined him in the ice carving business, working with his father to turn blocks of ice into works of art using chain saws, die grinders, flat chisels, and more specialized Japanese chisels. Campe rents freezer space, which allows him to work at his leisure and store finished items until they're needed for events. While he enjoys being with others while he's teaching and working alongside his son as they carve, he also likes the solitude of working alone.

"I put on my parka and hat and boots and gloves and I can disappear into the freezer and be by myself," he says. "It's quiet, it's always the same temperature in there, and nobody bothers me. It's sort of a nice place to work."

(continues)

(continued)

The amount of time necessary to complete a carving varies depending on its size and complexity. It takes Campe about an hour to carve a pair of kissing doves for a wedding, for instance. The price of each sculptor varies as well, but he says an average piece sells for $200.

While Campe very much enjoys his teaching job and doesn't plan to give it up to go into ice carving full time, he says he would have no trouble making a nice living from the trade.

"I could do only ice and make a lot of money," he says. "All my business comes from word of mouth, and I'm really busy. If I did a big marketing campaign and really worked at it, I could probably make a couple hundred thousand dollars a year. But I like the balance and variety that teaching provides."

If you're interested in becoming an ice carver, Campe advises, it's important to pick your location carefully. A small town or rural area may not have enough demand for ice carvings to keep a sculptor busy. However, the demand for ice sculpture seems to be increasing.

"Fifteen years ago, I don't know if Denver could have supported a full-time ice sculptor," Campe says. "But now it supports several of them. You just have to find the right location. There are a lot of people around the country who make a nice living carving ice."

Campe is so enjoying ice carving that he plans to extend his talents to other, more permanent mediums, such as marble, granite, wood, or bronze. "I have four kids," he says. "What I want to do is to make four, great pieces of art in lasting mediums so they each can have something that I made. You can make a really great ice sculpture, but you can't pass it along to your grandkids."

MOVIE SET CATERER

OVERVIEW

An army may travel on its stomach, but a film crew won't get much done either if it isn't fed well—and that's where the movie caterer comes in. Caterers to movie sets provide huge amounts of well-prepared food for the crews, production people, artists, actors, and executives.

When the call comes in, the caterer figures out exactly how many people will need to be served, what to prepare, and how to deliver. This isn't always easy, since a film set could be almost anywhere—up in the high deserts, out in the wilderness—but wherever the production goes, so must the food to feed the crew, executives, and talent.

Film caterers are often some of the hardest-working people on the set, typically getting up in the wee hours of the morning to start serving coffee, breakfast, snacks, lunch, and dinner to a crews of at least 150 people—and often many more. Most catering companies send out a mobile kitchen or some sort of equipped truck, including everything you'd find in a commercial kitchen tucked into a much smaller space. While there, the caterer is expected to handle all the prep, presentation, and cleanup for each meal—and then start all over again in a very short time. Typically, a movie set caterer can work at least 60 to 70 hours a week, sometimes up to 100 hours a week. To be successful, you need to have a lifestyle that can accommodate those kind of work

AT A GLANCE

Salary Range
Depends on size of company, but owners can earn from $50,000 up. Chefs who work for a caterer, earning union rates, may start at $21.99 per hour, but overtime is the norm rather than the exception, and daily earnings can range from $200 on a non-union shoot to $400 per day and more on a big production.

Education/Experience
Background in food service and cooking important.

Personal Attributes
The right kind of demeanor to handle enormous pressure and the film set environment, a varied background, ability to think quickly on your feet, professionalism and excellent communication skills

Requirements
Experience in food service, event planning, and cooking.

Outlook
Good. There are lots of opportunities but also lots of competition. Although there has been a slowdown affecting the film industry across North America, catering companies are still typically able to get as much work as they can handle.

binges, and the strength to be able to work twice as long as you sleep each day.

Still, movie set caterers do what they do because of the creativity and challenge the job entails. They have to be able to produce completely different meals every day for the whole run of the show—which is much different than churning out the same old menu entrees every night with an occasional special sprinkled in.

Movie catering companies need to be able to provide a large repertoire of food from all around the world, but because of the visibility, the catering staff gets to meet almost everyone working on the set. This provides far more visibility than a restaurant chef or cook would ever have in a traditional restaurant, with much more opportunity for positive feedback and appreciation. On a typical set, three hours after the first call the crew must have a substantial food break—more than a snack but less than a meal. Six hours after the first call, they must have a full hot sit-down meal. Most contracts stipulate that the caterer needs to have the meal ready 30 minutes before the scheduled time, but often the shooting runs late. Nevertheless, the caterer must be ready and have the food hot. Often, there is one eating area and menu for the extras, and another for the actors and crew.

If you're interested in preparing food and cooking, and you're thinking about a catering career, you can start by working as a server or an assistant for a caterer, and then work your way up to cooking for a catering company. Eventually, you can start your own catering company. Obviously, you'll need an interest in food and cooking, a keen sense of taste and smell, and you should enjoy developing new recipes and trying new ideas. You'll also need a good business sense, since you'll often be responsible for managing and leading the people you work with, estimating food requirements, and ordering supplies to keep the kitchen running smoothly. Many Hollywood caterers are also event planners, and can provide food for artists' tour buses and refreshments for dressing rooms.

Pitfalls

Catering for a movie set can be extremely nerve-wracking and stress-inducing. Things often go wrong, and you'll need to be able to come up with an alternative plan at the last minute when the bus breaks down or the waiters don't show up. Providing food for a set or film shoot is also a big responsibility because of union contracts, which stipulate hot food must be served at certain intervals or the employees earn a big bonus. Failing to provide food can thus cost a company big bucks if you fail to show up.

Given that the work is hard, the hours are long, and there are limited days off while in production, this job really isn't for everyone.

Perks

A career in film will always be a bit of a roller coaster ride whether you're behind a camera or a cooking pot. But if you love cooking and don't mind some sleepless nights, catering for the film industry may just be for you. Although the work is hard and the hours are long, a big part of what attracts people to the job is the money. If you love food and entertaining, and you don't mind the pressure, it can be lots of fun catering movie sets, commercial shoots, and other Hollywood events. Your days will always be different and there will always be new challenges.

Get a Jump on the Job

If you're thinking about a catering career, you should start out working at a local restaurant, learning how to serve food and interact with guests. See if you can get a job as a sous-chef or helper in the kitchen or a catering company, and watch how the chef handles the pressure. In college you can major in food science, hotel management, or home economics, or you can attend a culinary institute for more in-depth training.

Lisa Wallace, general manager of Behind the Scenes Catering

Have a 2 a.m. photo call or an overnight editing crew? It's no problem for Lisa Wallace and Behind the Scenes Catering—they'll pop on over right on time, bearing coffee and orange juice, as arranged.

"We do a lot more production work than commercial shoots," Wallace explains, "and almost all rock stars." In fact, since 1985, Behind the Scenes has been one of the country's best-known on-location catering companies for the TV, video, music, broadcast, and motion picture industries, as well as corporate and private clients. The company has provided on-site food for the dressing rooms of a range of high-octane clients, including Frank Sinatra, The Eagles, Bonnie Raitt, Van Halen, Harry Connick, Jr., Hootie and the Blowfish, Elton John, and Metallica. They've also handled planning services for events such as the 1995 America's Cup Broadcast Compound, the 1996 Republican National Convention Media Compound, the 1997 ESPN Winter/Summer X-Games, the NBC Olympic compounds at the 2000 Sydney Olympic Games, and many other on-location productions.

Typically, it all starts when the production manager of the show or event gives Wallace information about meal service requirements for the cast and crew, as well as details on the stars' requests about what they want in their dressing rooms. "I'm doing Snoop Dog at the moment," she says, "and he wants four bottles of Cristal champagne and 45 packs of Cigarellas to go on all the buses. You get the strangest requests!" she laughs. Van Halen requires some very specific items, including a case of Cranberry Kiwi-Lime Naturally Carbonated, three types of crackers, three large loaves of fresh-baked bread, and fresh organic vegetables for the juicer, kept on ice. "Stars can be very specific about what they want to eat and drink, what kinds of gourmet items." In fact, many of their clients have proven to be so interesting, the company has produced a book about their experiences: *Backstage Pass: Catering to Music's Biggest Stars* by owner John Crisafulli with Sean Fisher and Teresa Villa.

When Wallace provides food, it's always prepared on-site and includes beverage services, waste management, and restrooms. Tables, chairs, tents, trailers, mobile power and fencing can all be provided, and the company also provides advance information about local vendors and contacts.

How much food the company provides depends on the show, Wallace explains. A photo shoot, for example, can be a single day or may involve two weeks straight. "We may provide foods for the employees as well as foods that are going to be in the show itself as well as products to be shot on the set," she explains. "Productions are interesting," she adds. "When you're shooting commercials, you can end up in some really strange locations—like on a rock on the side of a hill. It presents a lot of logistical challenges, to be able to provide the best quality, freshest ingredients and endure unique conditions—it's challenging. You have to be extremely self-sufficient; typically there may be no chance for electricity or water."

To answer these challenges, Wallace maintains a fleet of vehicles including a couple of refrigerated box trucks to keep the food fresh. A typical gig involves a sequence of food

(continues)

(continued)

production. "First, you have to feed the production crews," she says. "They can come in a day or two in advance to prepare for the show. They want food, and if they're union they must be fed hot food at certain hours."

They stay on through the show, and then they load up and Wallace must continue feeding them. Then it's time to stock the buses for when the tour continues, which may involve providing food from restaurants all over town. "We're running all over and stocking buses."

Anyone interested in catering these big events and Hollywood productions should probably have a culinary background, Wallace says. "And you can take event planning and hospitality courses. It's always good to have an education. But really, what helps most is the ability to respond to emergencies, to pull off amazing things under pressure. That takes experience."

Wallace notes that the company doesn't have a lot of competition because they have the reputation and experience—and even more important, they understand how to deal with entertainers. "It's important having staff and management who aren't going to bother them, asking for autographs," she explains. "We respect their privacy—we just take care of service and keep them happy."

Wallace started out in the hotel/catering industry, working in various four- and five-star resorts for 15 years before moving on into event project management. "I was in Salt Lake City organizing for the Olympic Winter Games in 2002 for three years." She also went to Australia for the summer games, and managed the IOC hospitality there. "That led me to other projects," she says. "I worked with the White House and the First Lady, I met world leaders. I was at Sea Island Georgia last year. I did the inauguration in January, various balls, candlelight dinners, and smaller private parties." Owner John Crisafulli also catered the same Olympics, although the two were working in different areas and didn't meet at the time.

"This industry really attracts a certain type of person," she says. "I tried to do the typical 8 to 5, but it doesn't keep me interested. I really have a passion for what I do, and you have to, to stay in this business. The key is finding balance, a quality of life."

Easier said than done, because event catering to the stars can be very hard on the nerves. "It's very stressful and very time-consuming," Wallace says. "It's not a part-time business. You kind of live it and breathe it."

Each new job is always different, bringing a different environment, clients, their needs, the logistics. The only thing you can guarantee about celebrity catering is that something will always go wrong.

"You can spend three years planning an Olympics, and then you have 17 days of improvisation," Wallace laughs. "Maybe there's an avalanche and you can't get the food up the hill … things like that. Even if it's just a small dinner party, the truck breaks down—it's always something. Something is going to throw a wrench in your plans, no matter how well you prepare. How well you recover from that shows your true ability."

PASTRY CHEF

OVERVIEW

If you've always loved puttering around in your kitchen, creating cakes or puddings or your own ice cream, you may be interested in working as a pastry chef. Becoming a pastry chef requires patience, organization, and creativity in order to produce a finished dessert. In fact, pastry chefs are required to develop a set of unique skills.

As a pastry chef, you must be able to work solo or as part of a team, remember many different instructions, and work all kinds of hours. You should be creative, precise, and scientifically inclined, because science and technology will play a major role in your career. Unlike other forms of cooking, pastry and baking rely on the chemistry of the interaction of ingredients. Of course you need to be creative and artistic, but you also need to understand math, food science, and chemistry. Why does yeast rise best at a certain temperature? Why should some mixtures be mixed to add in air, and others not? Why does baking at high altitudes require recipe adjustments? As you can see, you'll need to know not just how to create dishes, but how to manipulate the functions of ingredients in baking to obtain the best result.

Every day, you must constantly plan and prepare, because almost every kind of pastry requires some advance preparation. You must start out by preparing the base ingredients—mixing sugar dough, croissant dough, puff pastry dough, and cookie dough; making cake batter and pouring it into to pans to be baked and frozen for

AT A GLANCE

Salary Range

$20,000 to more than $100,000, with an average of $50,000 a year. An entry-level pastry cook or helper will often make at least $8 an hour, a skilled assistant pastry chef will start at $25,000, and a corporate executive pastry chef can make upwards of $60,000 a year. The best salaries go to those with the most education, experience, and specialization.

Education/Experience

While a degree from a culinary school is not a requirement, it's the best way to get the skills and training. Alternatively, some pastry chefs get their training the hard way—starting from the bottom up and apprenticing to a chef. Although many successful chefs haven't gotten a formal culinary degree, the world of food service is becoming more competitive and professional. Today many executive-level positions in the industry require a degree. In management, a degree is nearly always a requirement.

Personal Attributes

Attention to detail, patience, flair, creativity, love of cooking, and an understanding of basic baking strategies.

Requirements

Some bakeries and restaurants may require a degree from culinary school or apprenticeship with a pastry chef. You'll also need to have a willingness to work hard, work long hours, and learn from mistakes.

Outlook

Jobs in all areas of food production are expected to increase by about 5 percent through 2012.

later use; cooking creams and icings with which to decorate; rolling out dough for tart shells or cookies, and so on.

But that's just the beginning. Next is the fun stuff—decoration! Customers will

Karen Carr, pastry chef

Whether it's breakfast croissants, pies, pastries, danish, cakes and cookies, or tiramisu, Karen Carr at Just Like Mom's in Weare, New Hampshire, can create it. Carr grew up being interested in cooking, and the idea of being a pastry chef was always in the back of her mind.

She learned her craft at the two-year College of Culinary Arts at Johnson and Wales University in Providence, Rhode Island, which cemented her desire to specialize in pastries. After graduation, her first job was making doughnuts at a small bakery; subsequently, she worked as a manager and a private chef.

She recommends that anyone interested in becoming a professional chef or pastry chef get some experience in restaurants. "You need to get your feet wet in the restaurant business at some level to see if it's for you," she explains, "because you're pretty much kissing goodbye every weekend and every holiday. It's just a different lifestyle—either you like it, or you don't."

Carr had been producing a wide variety of desserts and pastries from home before embarking on Just Like Moms in 2004; today, she has several full- and part-time employees. "I like the creativity, the decorating,' she explains. "My father says I'll never retire, because someone will always need a cake!"

be more likely to order items they find attractive—especially desserts.

There are several educational paths to choose from for a career in pastry arts, including attending a culinary institute for an associate or bachelor's degree in culinary arts. Many different programs offer classroom study and baking experience. One-year programs typically offer pastry courses that prepare you for an entry level position, whereas two-year associate degree and four-year bachelor's degree programs include both pastry courses and general education classes, together with electives that provide a more well-rounded education. Graduates of pastry programs are prepared for positions at any establishment with in-house baking and pastry operations, such as caterers, restaurants, hotels, and bakeries.

As a pastry chef, you'll be responsible for handling the money, the creative jobs, and the staffing oversight necessary for a

pastry kitchen, including staff training, menu planning, ordering, baking, and finishing desserts. You may consult with clients to determine their needs and dreams, especially for a big event like a wedding. Or, you may choose to give class demonstrations, be on television, or judge food shows. Whether you have a passion for creating imaginative pastries, a drive to develop new desserts, or the desire to manage a bakery, there are endless possibilities in the field of pastry making. If you work at a large hotel or restaurant, you may train the staff, coordinate with the sales departments as well as the support departments, and consult with clients to determine their needs and wants. Pastry chefs typically report to the executive chef, who serves as the boss of the entire kitchen.

Pastry chefs who own their own bakeries still need to consult with clients and know how to run their own businesses, hiring and training staff as needed.

Although education and schooling is important, many chefs believe the key is to apprentice with a top-notch pastry chef who can show you exactly what to do.

Pitfalls

You've got to enjoy early mornings, because no matter where you work, pastry chefs typically fire up the ovens at the break of day. You've also got to be comfortable with working nights and weekends, at least in the beginning if you work in restaurants or hotels. In addition, producing delicate, intricate pastries for someone's very special event—such as a wedding—can cause enormous stress.

Perks

Turning out perfect pies, cakes, and croissants can be an extremely creative and gratifying career. If you love food,

getting paid to create it can make for a wonderful lifestyle.

Get a Jump on the Job

If you're interested in becoming a pastry chef, the best thing you can do is to talk to chefs and bakers, go to the library and read about the culinary industry, study pastry cookbooks, and check out all the different schools and programs to determine which program will benefit you the most. You can start cooking at home at any age, so head right out in the kitchen and see what you can do. By about age 16 or 18 you can get a job in a local restaurant—a job in any capacity can give you a sense of what the industry is all about. As soon as possible, start working in the kitchen, and watch what the pastry chef does. Pick up as many tricks as you can. There are lots of courses available at local schools and sometimes from private chefs—try a course or two to see how you like it.

PIZZA MAKER

OVERVIEW

Pizza is sometimes called America's favorite food—and for good reason. Statistics tell us that on average, every man, woman, and child in America eats 46 slices of pizza a year!

There are lots of ways to indulge the pizza habit. You can buy a frozen pie at the grocery store, stick it on a baking sheet, and bake it in your oven. You can make your own dough by mixing flour, fresh yeast, water, and salt, and you can make your own sauce and grate your own cheese if you're really ambitious (or perhaps just have a lot of time on your hands).

For most of us, however, the best way to get a really good pizza is to go to the nearest pizza shop and buy one. If you ever wondered why pizzeria pizza looks and tastes better than what comes frozen in a box or out of your home oven, it has to do with several factors.

First, heavy-duty pizza ovens can reach higher temperatures than home ovens, and they're bigger—which means the air moving inside them has more room to circulate. This helps brown the crust and ensures a crispy texture.

The other reason is the pizza maker. A good pizza maker takes his or her work seriously, uses fresh ingredients, and pays attention to the details of the preparation.

Pizza makers work in various settings. There are privately owned pizzerias, some of which are handed down from generation to generation within a family. Some Italian restaurants hire pizza makers along with other cooks and chefs. Other

AT A GLANCE

Salary Range

The average salary for an experienced pizza maker is $10.50 an hour, according to government statistics. Many pizza makers make less than that, but professional pizza chefs who work in busy, high-profile restaurants in cities can make much more.

Education/Experience

There are no established educational requirements to be a pizza maker. There are pizza-making classes available at various locations, and some professional pizza makers are graduates of culinary schools or have completed culinary programs in vocational schools or career centers. If you aspire to own your own pizza shop, you should consider taking some business courses, or even earning a degree in business.

Personal Attributes

You'll need to be coordinated and able to think on your feet as you work, because you have to move quickly and surely when making and tossing pizza dough. You should be able to work well with co-workers, supervisors, and customers. Customers tend to be fascinated with the art of pizza making, so it helps if you're fairly outgoing and don't mind answering questions. You should also have good hygienic practices.

Requirements

Some restaurants require workers to get certification of good health before granting employment. If working in a restaurant, you'll need to follow the requirements of the health agencies that oversee the establishment.

Outlook

Jobs as pizza makers are expected to be particularly plentiful, as, according to U.S. pizza industry figures, the increase in pizza restaurants is higher than any other restaurant growth. Overall jobs for chefs, cooks, and food preparation workers are expected to increase by about 10 percent through that period, which is considered to be average job growth.

pizza makers work for chain pizza shops, such as Pizza Hut and Papa John's. Even some grocery stores hire pizza makers to prepare pies that customers can either eat in the store or take home and bake in their kitchens.

Pizza makers are usually responsible for making the dough, prepping ingredients to be used for toppings, and making sure everything necessary for making the pizza is in place. Some pizza parlors and restaurants make their own sauce, but many buy sauce in large cans from wholesale grocers. And, while some places do shred their own cheese, others buy it preshredded in large bags.

Once all the ingredients and tools are where they need to be, the pizza maker can get down to the actual business of stretching the dough into the proper-sized round, spreading it with just the right amount of sauce, and putting on the desired toppings. Some pizza makers put on a show as they stretch the crusts, spin them, and even throw them into the air.

An experienced pizza maker working in a popular restaurant or pizza shop normally will earn more than someone hired to work in a chain pizza restaurant or grocery store. If you own your own pizzeria, you have the potential to earn even more. Pizza in the past few years has gone upscale, moving out of pizza shops and into more trendy eating places. The standard pepperoni, sausage, and mushroom toppings have been joined by the likes of shredded duck breast, Greek olives, goat cheese, red onions—even hand-shucked clams.

If you think those toppings sound strange, however, you probably haven't heard about the newest pizzas being introduced in Japan, laden with toppings such as shrimp, squid, tuna, and mayonnaise on a seafood pizza, or shredded pork, shimeji mushrooms, bamboo shoots, and seaweed on the Japanese-style pie.

Some pizza makers like to impress customers with how quickly they can throw together a pie, while others insist that slow is the way to go.

One traditional, 68-year-old pizza maker interviewed recently by a reporter from the *New York Times* bemoaned the fact that pizza has become a fast food. He refuses to make his pizzas quickly, insisting they wouldn't be good if he did. Another New York City pizza maker is such a purist that he refuses to use any toppings on his pizza. He celebrates the fact that he can make something that tastes so good using just flour, water, and salt, much the way it was done 2000 years ago in Pompeii. Then there's the Phoenix pizza maker on a mission to get pizza chefs the respect he says they deserve but are only starting to receive. He works long hours, experimenting with combinations of toppings such as pistachio nuts, rosemary, and red onion—concoctions that recently earned him the prestigious James Beard Award naming him the best chef in the Southwest.

Not many pizza makers, however, can afford to work at their own pace, spend hours experimenting with topping combinations, or refuse to give customers a pie with toppings. As the popularity of pizza continues expand and more and more pizza restaurants open, the need for versatile, creative pizza chefs will continue to increase.

Ricardo Gallegon, pizza maker

Ricardo Gallegon of San Leone Pizza & Pasta in New York City has been making pizza for 20 years, and by now he figures he's got it just about right. Still, he says, someone just looking to get into the business shouldn't assume that it's easy. Not at first, anyway.

"You've got to learn the make the dough before you do anything else," Gallegon says. "And that can be tricky. There are different kinds of flour you could use, the yeast can vary, it even depends on how hard or soft the water is that you use."

Then, Gallegon says, just when you've perfected your dough, you might move to another pizza restaurant cnd find out they want you to make it differently. "It all depends on which place you work," he says. "All the places have their own way to make the dough." Once you've learned to make good dough and to stretch it properly, Gallegon says, the rest of the pizza making process is easy.

Gallegon's work hours are enviable for many who work in the restaurant business. He shows up at work at 10 a.m. each weekend, at which time he starts up the ovens, makes the dough, and preps other ingredients for the anticipated lunchtime rush. The pizzeria remains moderately busy all afternoon, but once the lunch crush has subsided, Gallegon has time to straighten up his work area and prep some more for the night shift, which comes in at 6 p.m. and works until 2 a.m.

"That's a good thing about working for this restaurant," Gallegon says. "There are two shifts, so you don't have to work the very long hours. Most of the time a pizza place will open early and stay open until 11 o'clock or so. And, that's when you end up working double shifts sometimes."

Gallegon was never formally trained as a pizza maker—he just learned on the job. You can go to a culinary school and be trained to work in an upscale pizza restaurant, he says, but that wasn't an option for him. Still, he says, he thinks he's done pretty well as a pizza maker, and he's pleased with his accomplishment of being able to make a cheese pizza in just 30 seconds. "I'm very fast," Gallegon says. "I can make the whole pizza, from start to finish, in 30 seconds. That's just half a minute to make a cheese pizza. So, does he toss the dough? "Oh, yes," he laughs. "I just let it fly."

Gallegon enjoys the job, and his favorite part is stretching and twirling the dough in front of the customers.

"You get to make the pizza in front of everyone, which is fun, because they can see how fast you can work and how clean you are," Gallegon says. "That's what I really like about my work. The customers get to appreciate the skill it takes to make a pizza the right way."

Pitfalls

While some pizza chefs in upscale restaurants are very well paid, the majority of pizza makers won't be getting rich any time soon. As with many other sorts of restaurant work, making pizza can entail long, irregular hours, require you to work on weekends and holidays, and cause you to spend long hours on your feet. Plus, pizza ovens bake at high temperatures, which can get pretty uncomfortable on a hot, summer afternoon. When you're just starting out as a pizza maker, you'll probably be called on for clean-up chores and other work that can get tiresome and tedious.

Perks

Making pizza tends to be a social job because the pizza maker is usually within sight of the customers and can interact with them and with fellow employees. If your employer allows you to, you can get creative with sauces and toppings, coming up with new combinations of ingredients. If you do well at making pizza, establish the proper contacts, and have enough ambition, you could eventually own your own restaurant.

Get a Jump on the Job

If you're old enough, get a job in a pizza shop or restaurant so you can watch to see how the pizza is made. Observe each step of the pizza-making process, from how the dough is made, to how the sauce and toppings are applied. You can also experiment with making pizza at home, including the dough. There are many ways to make pizza dough, so you'll benefit from trying a variety of recipes to see which one you like best. Look in a few different cookbooks, or online, to find some of the different dough recipes available.

PRODUCE BUYER

OVERVIEW

A produce buyer locates and orders the necessary fruits and vegetables for grocery stores; large discount stores such as Wal-Mart; wholesale produce distributors; and large hotels and restaurants. Some buyers oversee the purchase of produce for entire chains of grocery stores. While buying produce doesn't sound overly complicated, it requires knowledge, experience, and the ability to do some very good guesswork.

A produce buyer is responsible for making sure that the store, hotel, or restaurant he or she is responsible for gets the fruits and vegetables that it wants, when it wants them, and for the price it wants to pay for them. Sometimes, those tasks are nearly impossible.

That's because produce availability can be affected by weather, shipping problems, political unrest, and many other factors. Just because a produce buyer can buy mangoes for $14 a box one week, doesn't mean that they'll be available for that price the next week. Of course, you'll have a better chance of getting what you want if you're able to develop good relationships with vendors. It's helpful to get to know the vendors you buy from, so that you can establish mutual trust and understand how each other works. This allows you to effectively negotiate prices and transportation arrangements, assuring that you'll get the best quality produce available at the best possible prices.

AT A GLANCE

Salary Range

The average salary for a produce buyer is $50,385, with the bottom 25 percent earning less than $43,995, and the top 25 percent earning more than $59,723. The salary generally depends on factors such as the size of the employer, employee credentials and experience, and location.

Education/Experience

There are no established educational requirements to be a produce buyer, but some employers would prefer a college degree in agriculture or a related field. Others might be interested in an employee who has a business background. Still others require that an employee has completed high school and has several years of working experience.

Personal Attributes

Buying produce is a fairly complex business that requires much attention to detail and the ability to make decisions based on a number of interacting factors. While you don't need to be a rocket scientist to be a produce buyer, you must be able to consider facts and use them in making decisions. It also helps to be in good physical condition, because you'll no doubt find yourself hoisting boxes of bananas and watermelons. You need to be able to communicate effectively with suppliers, other employees, and supervisors, and you should be able to manage your time well, as you'll have a variety of tasks to complete each day.

Requirements

Some employers require any employees who handle food to have regular physical examinations to make sure they don't have any illnesses that could be spread to customers.

Outlook

As the variety of produce that's available in grocery stores continues to expand, the need for good produce buyers will increase. These jobs are expected to increase by about 10 percent by 2012, which is considered average job growth.

In addition to ordering fruits, vegetables, and perhaps miscellaneous items such as birdseed, salad toppers, vegetable dips, and salad dressings, a produce buyer is responsible for checking orders when they arrive to make sure the items are in good condition. If they are, you'll authorize payment of the invoice. If the shipment is damaged or spoiled, however, you'll need to determine who is responsible for the problem, and how you're going to replace the order you can't use.

Many produce buyers have faced such nerve-wracking experiences as getting a load of watermelons delivered just before the Fourth of July holiday, only to find

Jim Hickey, produce buyer

A produce buyer for a chain of 36 grocery stores and 11 convenience shops, Jim Hickey has learned how to deal with unexpected problems and situations.

"Everything is different, every day," Hickey says. "It's a matter of controlled chaos, because you never know what you'll be dealing with. It's a very fast-paced job, and there are a lot of unknowns."

Hickey spends three days a week in the grocery chain's distribution center in eastern Pennsylvania. There, he communicates with the managers of each store to assess their current inventories and needs, accepts or rejects deliveries, determines and places orders, figures out how much to charge for various items, oversees invoice payments, studies sales trends and figures, and performs many other necessary tasks.

He also works hard to keep up with weather and other extenuating circumstances around the globe that might affect the availability and price of produce.

"A crop that's held back just three to five days by cold weather can throw everything off," Hickey says. "It gets crazy when you pay $25 one week for a case of beans, the price goes down to $16 the next week, and then it's back up to $24 the week after that."

And, he says, while you can be watchful and try to plan the best you can, there will always be some surprises.

"Rain in California can stop our supply of strawberries in Pennsylvania," Hickey says. "We're very much slaves to Mother Nature. The weather pretty much dictates it all."

Other factors, such as shipping problems, also can cause headaches, he says.

Whenever possible, Hickey tries to order directly from the grower. He can pick up the phone, for instance, place an order with Grimmway Carrots in California, and at the same time, hire a truck to bring the carrots to Pennsylvania. That kind of convenience, he says, is the result of a lot of relationship building.

"We work hard to develop relationships with the growers," he says. "I can call somebody at the vineyards who I can count on to give me good information and advice about which grapes to buy. That makes a big difference."

(continues)

(continued)

On two days every week, Hickey drives a truck about an hour and a half to the Philadelphia Terminal Market, a wholesaler from which Hickey can buy the more unusual items that he needs only in limited quantities. He usually leaves at about 2 a.m. and arrives at the market by 3:30. Going at that time, he says, allows him to avoid city traffic and get the best produce selection.

He might return with *jicama*, a member of the potato family that's very popular among Latin Americans; Habanero peppers; Swiss chard; Italian eggplant; and artichokes to satisfy the wants of the populations served by the grocery chain.

Market workers with whom he's become acquainted help him select fruits and vegetables. And, the market lists current prices each day on its Web site, allowing him to determine ahead of time what, and how much, he'll purchase.

By 7 a.m., Hickey is ready to get in the truck and return to the distribution center, where he'll arrange for the produce he's just purchased to be sent to the various stores.

Hickey has a lot of work experience in the grocery business, but his education is in computer science. He started working at a grocery store when he was 14, pushing shopping carts in from the parking lot. He worked his way up to the produce department, and found that he enjoyed working there. After finishing high school and earning a college degree in computer science, he worked at a wholesale produce distributor for a while before joining the grocery store chain. "I can't seem to get away from produce," Hickey says.

The computer training is not being wasted, however. Hickey developed a software program that the grocery chain uses to keep track of availability, supply, orders, and other records.

Hickey has no regrets concerning his career choice. In fact, he's very happy doing what he does. He's had the opportunity to travel to Spain to see how Clementines (a small citrus fruit) grow, to Chile and Mexico to check out grape production, and to California to visit cherry producers.

"I've had some good opportunities, and I like that I don't know exactly what the day will hold when I get up every morning," Hickey says. "It's satisfying to go home at the end of the day and know that I've done what needs to be done."

they've arrived in a freezer truck and are frozen solid. Or, opening an anticipated box of cherries, only to find that the vendor has sent apricots, instead.

A produce buyer in some cases must determine the selling price for produce that comes in. This is true more often for buyers for grocery or wholesale stores than it is for those who buy for hotels and restaurants. What makes the pricing job tricky is that grocery stores often advertise specials the week before they run, and the prices need to be set even before that so that there's time to get the sales sheets printed and distributed to shoppers. A produce buyer may have to venture a guess on what something is going to cost two or three weeks before it even arrives at the store. Imagine what happens if, as a produce buyer, you assure your boss that California strawberries are plentiful and can be put on sale for $2.50 the week after next, only to have the crop nearly wiped out a few days later by torrential downpours and hail in the Golden State. In addition, you've got to keep an eye on what your competition is doing as far as sale prices go.

As customers get used to being able to buy a large selection of fruits and vegetables year round, they're likely to become more demanding about what they want on the shelves of their grocery stores and the menus of their favorite restaurants.

People are exposed to produce that even five years ago wasn't readily available, and they quickly become used to having it and expect that it will be continually present. A produce buyer must keep up with consumer trends and demands, as well as changing population demographics within the area.

If an area suddenly sees an influx of Asian residents, for instance, the produce buyer will need to determine what additional items he or she may need to order. Customers are pretty good about making their wishes known, but it helps if the buyer can anticipate what they'll ask for.

A produce buyer must be organized and well versed enough with computers to use them to organize and locate inventory, operate spreadsheets, and so forth. You also need to be able to manage employees, as well as provide effective reports to your supervisor or supervisors.

Pitfalls

Because of the nature of the job, you may sometimes find yourself responsible for a buy that turned out badly due to circumstances that are beyond your control. And, you could find yourself dealing with an irate customer who absolutely must have red, yellow, and orange bell peppers for that evening's dinner party, when you were only able to get red and yellow delivered that day.

Perks

Buying produce is challenging, but it's an interesting job that changes every day. It also enables you to be at the forefront of produce trends as well as being the first person in town to know about a new variety of orange being imported from the Mediterranean.

Get a Jump on the Job

Begin learning everything you can about produce. Find out how different fruits and vegetables are used, who eats them, how they grow, where they grow, how much they cost, and if there are different varieties of them. Read books about growing fruits and vegetables, and cookbooks to learn how they can be used. Visit the produce department of your local grocery store often to see what's in stock, how much it costs, and how fresh it looks. Strike up a conversation with the produce workers. They should be able to tell you where the fruits and vegetables come from, when they arrived in the store, and other information. When you're old enough, you can apply for a job in the grocery store and ask to be stationed in the produce department.

RESTAURANT REVIEWER

OVERVIEW

While some people barely notice what they're eating, other people are fascinated with all of the many aspects of food and dining. It's the second group that supports the job of restaurant reviewing—the collective presentation of information about food and restaurants that appears every day in newspapers, magazines, books, and online publications.

Restaurant reviewers review restaurants, travel to different parts of the world to explore their cuisine, write about people who work in the food industry, predict upcoming food trends, and cover many more areas concerning food. Some specialize, or find a niche topic that they write about often or exclusively. Well-known restaurant reviewers Jane and Michael Stern, for instance, crisscross the United States searching for old-fashioned soda fountains, standout diners, barbecue joints, soul-food restaurants, and drive-ins, and then write about what they find in a monthly column in *Gourmet* magazine called "Road Food."

Another restaurant reviewer might specialize in exploring and reporting different wines, and how they pair with various foods. Another may only write profiles on hot, new chefs and restaurants.

Most, however, cover a variety of food-related topics. If you work for a newspaper or magazine, you'll have an editor who will assign you stories. Once you've proven yourself, you'll probably be encouraged to come up with your own

AT A GLANCE

Salary Range

The average annual earnings for salaried writers and authors is about $43,000. A freelance food writer can earn anywhere from $50 for an article written for a small, local newspaper, to $6,000 for a series of articles for a high-profile publication. The wide range in the salaries of food writers depends on the circumstances of employment, the writer's experience and celebrity, and other factors.

Education/Experience

Being a food writer typically requires a degree in journalism, writing, English, or a related field. Some culinary training and experience would also be helpful. Some culinary schools offer weeklong workshops in food writing. One school that does is the Culinary Institute of America in Hyde Park, New York. You can find out more about the workshop at http://www.ciachef.edu.

Personal Attributes

You'll need to have a strong interest in food—but not just in eating it. Restaurant reviewers need to be well versed in food trends, international topics that affect the food industry, agricultural issues, and so forth. You'll also need strong writing skills, the ability to express yourself well in your writing, and the ability to develop story ideas and present them to editors and publishers. Restaurant reviewers normally deal with other people, so you should be personable and have a neat appearance.

Requirements

You'll need to have some writing samples, even if it's from a school newspaper or online publication. You'll also need a contact list of publications that might be interested in hiring you to write a food story.

Outlook

Writing jobs are expected to increase by between 10 and 20 percent through the year 2012. That job growth is considered to be average. Web-based publications may add opportunities for restaurant reviewers.

ideas for stories. You also probably will be responsible for coming up with ideas for photos to accompany those stories.

If you're writing on a freelance basis, you'll need to come up with ideas that you can pitch to editors at newspapers or magazines. Once you've established some connections, a publication might ask you to take on an assignment. When you're pitching an idea for a story, it's very

Steven Shaw, food writer

Many people refer to Steven Shaw as a restaurant reviewer. While he has, in fact, written more than 200 reviews of New York City restaurants and eats about $20,000 worth of restaurant meals each year, he prefers to be called a food writer or food journalist.

After all, he says, he has written about many food-related topics for magazines, newspapers, and online publications, including *Elle, Saveur,* and *Food & Wine* magazines; the *New York Times* and the *National Post;* and Salon.com, Citysearch.com, and NYMetro.com. Shaw also has written a book called *Turning the Tables: Restaurants from the Inside Out,* and has another one in the works called *The Menu New York City.*

Shaw, who also runs a Web site called Fat-Guy.com on which he posts reviews, didn't start out as a food writer. His first career, actually, was that of a promising young lawyer in a Manhattan law firm. Shaw grew up in a family who liked to eat, but they didn't have enough money to go out to eat very often. It wasn't until he'd started his legal career that Shaw discovered fine dining—and how much he loved it.

Because his work involved a lot of lunches and dinners with clients, Shaw was able to explore the many great restaurants of New York City. Soon, he was writing reviews of the place in which he dined and e-mailing them to other lawyers in his firm. Colleagues started coming to him for advice on where to take important clients to dinner, and Shaw was happy to share his opinions.

Before he knew it, Shaw was more interested in writing about food and restaurants than in being a lawyer who was expected to work 80 hours a week. He could not, however, afford to leave behind his legal career to work full time at writing. For three years he remained at the law firm, while at the same time working to establish himself as a food writer. He posted restaurant reviews on his Web site and submitted articles and reviews to papers and magazines.

By 1996, he'd built up enough contacts and felt so confident that he could make it financially that he left his job as a lawyer to become a full-time food writer. Now, he happily writes about food—and also gets to spend more time with his family and friends.

Shaw works strictly on a freelance basis, because it gives him more flexibility and control over what he does. "I prefer to be a freelancer because it keeps things interesting," he says. "Instead of going to the same job every day, my job constantly changes based on whatever assignment I'm working on. Being a freelancer also allows me to make my own

(continues)

(continued)

schedule, so if I want to work on a few weekends and then take a week off to travel with my family, I can do that."

While Shaw enjoys all types of food writing, he especially likes writing about people who work in the food business. When he was working on his book about restaurants, for instance, he spent several weeks hanging out, watching the chefs work. "I spent a lot of time in the kitchens," he says. "And it was great, because I saw a lot and learned a lot. Then I tried to share that experience in writing with my readers."

He also enjoyed a stint a couple of summers ago when he spent several weeks traveling across Canada in search of country's best food for a series of articles for the *Montreal Gazette.*

Shaw, who comes by his "Fat Guy" moniker honestly, loves to eat. But, he says, food writers have to be aware of the many issues connected with food, and be able to look past the plate when it comes to writing.

"Food is endlessly fascinating, because it's about much more than just what's on the plate," Shaw says. "It's all about the people who cook it, serve it, grow it, transport it, sell it, and write about it. So many of the most important issues of the day come back to food: health, nutrition, the environment, labor, economics . . . food is part of all of those things."

While Shaw considers himself a lucky man, with possibly the best job in the world, he warned that food writing isn't always a walk in the park. In some years, he spends as much as four months traveling. And, although he enjoys travel, he says it is exhausting, and takes him away from his family for more time than he would like.

"I don't do all that traveling at once, but if you add up the days and week I spend on the road, it's a lot of time. I love it, but it's exhausting."

And sometimes, you have to be willing to pull out all the stops to meet your deadlines. "It's not all fun and games," Shaw says. "Once, in order to meet two different deadlines, I had to drive 1,000 miles in just two days." Still, he says, food writing is a great career. He recommends that someone interested in becoming a food writer should read and write about food as much as possible. Read the local newspaper's food section, cookbooks, and food magazines, he advised. And get some experience writing about food by talking to other people and writing about what they tell you.

"You can ask your grandparents about what they ate while they were growing up and write about that," he says. "Or talk to your parents about their favorite restaurants and write about it. Learning to write is all about practice."

Shaw spends a lot of time sampling food in fancy restaurants. His favorite foods, however, are not complicated dishes with unpronounceable names and fancy sauces. When asked about his favorite meal, Shaw was quick with a response. "Pizza," he says "I could eat pizza every day for breakfast, lunch, and dinner. But it has to be good pizza."

important that you do it in an organized and professional manner.

Research the publication you wish to contact and obtain a copy of their writer's guidelines. You usually can find these on the Web site of the publication. Once you've determined the guidelines, write a query letter in which you introduce your idea. Be careful, however, that you don't give so much information about your story that the editor can simply turn around and assign it someone on staff who happens to be looking for something to do. You want to share just enough information so that the editor wants to learn more.

The query letter also should include your full name and contact information, including your e-mail address. You should state whether your story will include recipes and/or photos. If you do plan to provide recipes, they'll need to be original, or adapted from other sources. You can't just reprint recipes from a cookbook or Web site.

Remember that magazines work well in advance—sometimes as much as a year. It won't do for you to submit a great idea for a Thanksgiving story in August—unless you're intending for it to run the following Thanksgiving.

While high-profile restaurant reviewers may have more work than they can handle, food writing can be challenging to break into. You may have to have a back-up job while you establish contacts and build up a resume.

Pitfalls

Food writing can involve significant travel, which can be considered as either a pitfall or a perk, depending on your circumstances. It can be a difficult field to break into, and you might not earn much initially.

Perks

If your circumstances are such that extensive traveling is a joy rather than a burden, you're likely to enjoy that aspect of food writing. Even if you don't get to travel, though, you'll be writing about topics that you find interesting and working with other people who share your interests.

Get a Jump on the Job

Start reading and writing about food as much as possible. Read some restaurant reviews to get an idea of how they're written, and then write your own review of your local pizza joint. Offer to review restaurants on a regular basis for your school newspaper, or set up a Web site where you post reviews, recipes, cooking tips, and so forth.

Keep an eye out for interesting goings-on in your area regarding food. If you hear about a new farmer in the area who's growing organic Swiss chard and selling it to the best restaurants in New York City, for instance, call the features editor at your local newspaper and offer to write about it. Even if the editor prefers to have a staff writer do the story, you will have established yourself as a creditable source.

Watch food shows on television to get an idea of what chefs are cooking and the techniques they're using. Read cookbooks, food stories in magazines and newspapers, and on Internet food sites.

SCHOOL NUTRITIONIST

OVERVIEW

If you think all a school nutritionist does is plan meals, keep reading. The job of a school nutritionist is incredibly varied, and involves a great amount of responsibility. In some schools, the nutritionist is expected to do just about everything but actually cook the meals.

Although responsibilities vary from school district to school district, a school nutritionist generally is expected to oversee the food service program and its staff. In a very large school district, this could mean being responsible for hundreds of staff members.

Most school lunch programs are federally subsidized, which means that the government pays a portion of food costs. As with most government programs, however, the school lunch program is subject to quite a few rules and requirements, all of which the nutritionist is expected to understand and abide by. All meals served in schools must meet certain guidelines set by the U.S. Department of Agriculture (USDA), including restrictions on the percentage of calories contained in the meal that come from fat (30 percent) and the percentage of total calories that come from saturated fat (10 percent).

As a school nutritionist, you're responsible for making sure the latest dietary guidelines are being met. If they aren't, your school could lose its government funding—and that wouldn't make your supervisors very happy.

AT A GLANCE

Salary Range

The average salary for a school nutritionist is about $42,000, according to government statistics; salaries range from $25,500 to more than $59,000. Salary varies according to job location, level of education, and certification.

Education/Experience

You'll need at least a bachelor's degree in a health and nutrition-related field. Chemistry, math, psychology, biology, English, anatomy, and sociology courses may be required as well. A degree in institutional food service may be acceptable, but you'll need a concentration in the area of nutrition.

Personal Attributes

School nutritionists must be versatile, able to think on their feet, and make quick decisions when problems arise. The very nature of the job—serving multiple meals that meet government guidelines day after day—makes it almost impossible to avoid glitches. You must be able to work independently while remaining accountable to other school personnel. Obviously, you should enjoy working with food and have a strong interest in health and nutrition.

Requirements

Requirements vary from state to state and among school districts, as well. Some school nutritionists are required to be registered dietitians, which means, in addition to an undergraduate degree that's approved by the American Dietetic Association, you'd need to pass the association's registered examination for dietitians. Or you may need to become a certified nutritionist, which means you must hold a bachelor of science degree in nutrition science from an accredited school, and pass a series of exams by the National Institute of Nutritional Education.

(continues)

AT A GLANCE *(continued)*

Outlook

Jobs for school nutritionists are expected to grow at an average rate between now and 2012, according to the Department of Labor's Bureau of Labor Statistics. While there's growing interest in and concern over nutrition in general, many schools are contracting food service companies to handle their food needs and thereby eliminating the need for on-site school nutritionists.

Figuring out government regulations concerning meals served is one thing. Selecting menus that kids will actually eat and enjoy is quite another. School food service has undergone some significant changes in the past decades, as nutritionists try to balance nutritional needs and guidelines, the changing tastes of students, financial considerations, and pressure to address the growing problem of obesity among children and teens.

As if all the work that goes into planning and serving meals isn't enough, school nutritionists often are expected to attend school board meetings; track food consumption, costs, profits and losses; and participate in collective bargaining processes when it comes time to renegotiate contracts. As a school

Patricia Anthony, school nutritionist

Pat Anthony has watched food trends come and go over the 22 years she's put in as a school nutritionist. She's kept up with government guidelines and recommendations, tried to keep a handle on food costs, and planned more menus that most of us probably do in a lifetime. And, although admitting her job is overwhelming at times, she still enjoys coming to work every day.

"I've found this to be a very rewarding career," Anthony says. "The people I've worked with have been just wonderful, and there's always something different going on. You never get bored, that's for sure."

Anthony, who has an undergraduate degree in food service and institutional management, also is a registered dietician, which requires additional schooling and training. She must constantly keep up with continuing education requirements in order to retain her certification, which keeps her up-to-date and on top of industry developments. "As a professional industry group, we encourage everyone to keep up with changing regulations," Anthony says.

A normal day for Anthony begins when she arrives at school at about 7:30 a.m. She makes sure everything is going smoothly for that day's food preparations, and then settles in her office to tackle a never-ending list of tasks necessary to keep a food service program running seamlessly for nearly 6,000 students.

She must make sure all the necessary supplies have been ordered, prepare written specifications for purchases, review bids from suppliers, and coordinate and administer the federal free and reduced-price lunch programs.

(continues)

nutritionist, you also might be responsible for coordinating the purchase, receipt, and storage of food, and even be called upon to present nutritional information and programs to students in classrooms and assemblies.

(continued)

Depending on the time of year, she may work on preparing a food service budget, a process for which Anthony says a crystal ball would be useful. "You need to try to project what will be happening in the marketplace, and how it will affect the food prices," she says. "That can be tricky."

Menu planning, which Anthony accomplishes with the help of special software that calculates nutrient standards for different age groups, is another weighty task she must accomplish regularly. She also oversees the accounting procedures of her office; supervises the special dietary needs of students who are diabetic, have food allergies, or other considerations; and hires, trains, and evaluates employees.

She's also been known to duck in to a classroom to talk to students about nutrition and health, and regularly provides educational materials regarding nutrition to teachers.

As if that's not enough, she and her staff of 91 also cater events ranging from sports banquets to special school board meetings on a regular basis. "We do about $100,000 worth of catering a year here," Anthony says. "We handle all kinds of events—whether they be for two people or 600 people." Anthony often oversees the banquets, which means it's not unusual for her to work evenings or weekends. If there's not an event to be catered, she usually heads for home at about 4:30 p.m.

In her experience, Anthony says, school nutritionists come into the job on two different pathways. One group starts out working in some capacity in a school food service program. Someone might work on a serving line, be a baker or cook, or a cashier. He or she discovers a strong interest in the field while working, and decides to pursue the education necessary to advance.

The other group intentionally sets out to enter the career field by studying nutrition or food service. Members of that group may also need to work in other positions within school food service before they advance to school nutritionist. Nutritionists also are needed for food service programs in hospitals, assisted living centers, and other institutions.

While the traditional route was to begin working in the field and advance up through the ranks, more and more people are earning degrees in nutrition or a related field and then seeking a job.

"We do have an increasing number of individuals who are coming in with nutrition degrees," Anthony says. "But others are still working their way up through the ranks."

Anthony reiterated that the work of a school nutritionist—also sometimes called a food service director—is varied and demanding. It requires not only knowledge of nutrition and food service, she says, but sound business capabilities, as well. And, the ability to work with others and get along with people is vital.

"You're constantly interacting with others," Anthony says. "If you can't do that successfully, it will be very hard for you to succeed in this job."

A school nutritionist must be willing and able to wear many hats, to keep up with ever-changing restrictions and guidelines, and work with a variety of people ranging from dishwashers to school management and government representatives. Unlike teaching positions, many school nutritionist jobs are 12-month contracts.

If you enjoy being challenged, however, and you're genuinely interested in helping kids get healthier and stemming the predicted obesity-related health problems, a school nutritionist position might be a perfect fit for you.

Pitfalls

In some school districts around the country, traditional in-house school lunch programs are being replaced with outside food service contractors, who sometimes can provide meals more efficiently and for less money. If this trend continues, openings for school nutritionists could decline. Also, school nutritionists tend to be on call pretty much around the clock to deal with problems that arise during non-school hours.

Perks

School nutritionists have a lot of responsibility and are important in the structure of a school district. Many school districts pay for personnel to further their education, which means you may be able to achieve advanced degrees with few out-of-pocket costs.

Get a Jump on the Job

You can learn a lot about the job of a school nutritionist by carefully observing the meals that are served in your school. Learn more about nutritional requirements for school meals by visiting the USDA's National School Lunch Program Web site at http://www.fns.usda.gov/cnd/Lunch/default.htm; then try to understand how the meals at your school meet those requirements. Read all that you can about nutrition, health, and meal planning. Try to get to know your school's nutritionist, and ask if he or she might have a few minutes sometime to talk to you about the job.

SOMMELIER

OVERVIEW

If you've ever gone to a restaurant and noticed an extensive wine list with a dizzying array of choices, you'll understand why fine restaurants like to offer their diners the services of a *sommelier*—the French word for wine steward or cellar master.

Sommeliers are specialists in wine service, and they're expected to have a broad knowledge about wines from all over the world. But it's not just wines you need to know about if you're going to be a sommelier—you also must understand how a certain wine would clash or complement a certain dish. At the same time, your advice needs to be delivered with poise and professionalism, so you need to be comfortable in dealing with the public.

When customers in an upscale restaurant want to order a bottle of wine with dinner, they may be overwhelmed by or unfamiliar with the selections offered on the wine list. When this happens, they ask the sommelier for advice. Many patrons are easily intimidated by wines and don't understand the terminology used to describe them, so the sommelier must be ready to coax from them a description of what they are looking for, and be understanding of budgetary limits. Typically, sommeliers love wine and are eager to share their knowledge, describing the regions, grapes, vineyards and vintages of all the wines on the restaurant's list. Even those diners who are knowledgeable about wine can benefit from advice, because the sommelier has tasted the

AT A GLANCE

Salary Range
Average starting salary is $14,000; for established sommeliers, the salary may range from $24,000 to more than $60,000, plus tips.

Education/Experience
Restaurant experience as a waitperson is helpful, followed by several years of experience working as an apprentice sommelier; a degree in enology or wine production may be helpful; courses and a diploma as a Master Sommelier is the highest degree possible.

Personal Attributes
Sommeliers love fine wines and fine dining, and have a genuine interest in sharing that knowledge with others. You should have a neat clean appearance, a well-spoken manner, an ability to work as a member of team, and a pleasant way with patrons.

Requirements
An extensive knowledge of wines and cellar management.

Outlook
Fair. Jobs are located throughout the country but are typically plentiful in large cities and tourist areas. Many smaller restaurants do not use the services of a sommelier, preferring the owner or manager to handle the wine chores. However, an increasing interest and sophistication about wines among the American public ensure that jobs in fine restaurants and hotels will continue. Since World War II, wine consumption in the United States has grown; the American vineyard has matured and some vineyards in California produce excellent wine. This has created a demand for sommeliers: Given the complexities and the cost of wines, many people recognize the need for guidance in choosing one. While employment growth will account for many new jobs, the overwhelming majority of openings will arise from the need to replace the high proportion of workers who leave the occupations each year.

items on the wine list and knows which wines go best with which entrees.

When the guests select a wine, the sommelier brings it to the table with the appropriate glasses and pours it for the customer to taste. The sommelier should encourage the patron to smell the wine first and should describe its components to him, bringing the wine to life for the patron before it even touches the palate. Sommeliers also decant wines, when necessary. (Decanting, usually done to red wines aged over ten years, is the process of pouring the wine into a decanter before serving it. This is done to allow the wine to breathe and to separate it from any sediment that may have settled at the bottom of the bottle.)

Extensive and frequent travel is part of the sommelier's job description. Many travel yearly to different regions to choose wines for their restaurant. At times, they will leave a promising wine behind, but return to it repeatedly until they feel it has aged properly.

Typically, sommeliers are at the top of the service heap in a restaurant, and may even advise chefs and the maître d'. Sommeliers usually create the wine list and manage both the list and the cellar. They are responsible for choosing the "house" wines, and they are expected to find the best suppliers for good inexpensive wines and the higher-priced vintages. They are able to assess wines for taints and other problems, and recommend wines that suit the customer's tastes and price range. In addition, a good sommelier can play a key role in getting his or her restaurant noticed, and can greatly enhance the eatery's reputation.

In most restaurants, the sommelier will both recommend and serve wines to patrons. After many years of experience, some sommeliers may consult for several restaurants, while others work exclusively with a single restaurant.

Many experienced sommeliers also consider that marketing wines for their restaurant to be an important part of the job, and host special wine-tasting dinners or wine tastings to help educate their patrons. Most also schedule special wine tastings for the restaurant's wait staff.

One good way to learn about being a sommelier is to start as a waitperson, learning how to handle customers and learning about food and service. Then you can move on to become an apprentice to a sommelier; working under another sommelier's guidance is the best way to learn. Usually, people enter this profession because they enjoy wines and want to learn more about them.

Most sommeliers work their way up to larger, finer restaurants, learning more about wine at every opportunity. After about five years, most sommeliers graduate to working independently. Eventually, after working many years in the business, a good sommelier has usually acquired a reputation and may be quoted in magazines and journals as an authority on wine. Some sommeliers consult for several restaurants, bringing their own flair to each house, while others choose to focus on a single restaurant where they are employed full time or in which they may share a financial interest. Experienced sommeliers also may host wine-tasting dinners, write a column for specialty magazines such as *Wine Spectator,* or act as mentors to aspiring

Heidi Gable, sommelier

Married to the chef at Donecker's Restaurant in Ephrata, Pennsylvania, it was probably inevitable that Heidi Gable took her degree in hotel/restaurant management and, after spending years working in restaurants, evolved into a sommelier.

"My husband and I shared an interest in going out to eat as consumers, and we had a lot of opportunities to try nice food and wines," Gable says. "My interest just continued to grow. I think you always mark those wonderful dinners with the right wine and great food. It sparks your curiosity." Largely self-taught, Gable has an extensive wine library at home. As a sommelier, she says her job "never gets soggy. There's always things to learn and try."

Gable admits that working in the restaurant business means throwing normal workday hours out the window. "It's not like you get up at 7 a.m., you make your money, and then go home and leave the worries of the job behind. Maybe I wouldn't like this job so much if I was with a different employer, but Donecker's is very good to me."

She's able to do most of her work at home, but finds it challenging to keep up with her deadlines. "The bigger the cellar, the harder it is," she admits. She does all of her bookwork, inventory, updates, and sending from home, and goes in to the wine cellar once a week to keep it neat and clean. "There's a lot of work in physically keeping a cellar of their size in order," she says. "Everything has to be organized according to country, to varietal, more distinctive geographic locations, according to vintage. We're proud to take people to see the cellar. They appreciate the effort we put into storing our wines properly."

As part of her job, she also constantly meets vendors and wine makers at her home office. "It's a lot of work—it isn't really the glamorous job it might seem to be. The wine cellar at Donecker's has more than 900 bottles. With that type of inventory, upkeep, bookkeeping, updating, pricing, you have to really have your eye and nose into what needs to be done." Gable also edits and publishes the wine list herself at home—no small feat, considering the list is about 45 pages long. In addition, she is constantly reordering, keeping the vintages up to date. Every week she makes corrections to the list, noting which wines are on order and thus are "temporarily unavailable," and which ones are no longer obtainable.

Friday and Saturday nights find her at the restaurant, where she consults and pours all the wine.

In addition, part of her job is to feature new wines, so Gable spends time thinking about how she will introduce them and present them to the public. She's begun "chef tastings" where she pairs wines with a seven-course dinner with different foods. She also changes the wine-by-the-glass types in late fall and late spring. That's when the new menus are printed, and Gable has the whole staff in to let them taste the new wines. "A lot of the staff really take an interest in the wine," she says.

"I enjoy wines from lesser-known parts of the world. I have to find ways to present them to the public where they'll be enjoyed and be reordered." Most of the wines are bought ready to drink, with most wine prices in the $20 to $70 range, although it's also possible to find a bottle ranging from $800 to $2,500. "It doesn't have to be a special occasion to drink wine," Gable says. "You can come in and get a nice bottle that is going to be good and that won't break your pocketbook. "

Gable advises students who might be interested in wine to begin by working in a restaurant. "Don't just jump right into doing wines," she says. "You can go to college to study wines and winemaking, but the growth comes from having the opportunity to try a lot of wine, and to pay attention and to make notes, to learn the geography of what you're tasting, to be able to start a wine vocabulary. If you get into a restaurant that puts a lot of effort into its wine program, the opportunities will be there if you show an interest."

"We meet great people—it's like having a second family at the restaurant," Gable says. "I look forward to seeing return customers I know. When I find a particular wine, I think: 'Oh, they're going to love this one!' It's a huge deal of fun working with the public in this. When I'm working on the floor it's a blast. Our customers are there to have a good time, and I'm very confident between our food and the wine that they leave enjoying everything."

sommeliers. Having a lifestyle instead of just a job, nearly all sommeliers say they are very much satisfied with their career.

Some sommeliers go to school for a degree in enology; others take courses given by professional associations (see Appendix A). Typically, these courses are designed to give a balanced academic and tasting introduction to the major wine styles and regions. The courses usually include basic training in wine tasting as well as key features of labeling laws, grape varietals, viticulture, and vinification. More involved courses may delve into growing wines, and may get into more details about elements of service and blind tasting techniques.

The truly dedicated may pursue the Master Sommelier degree, the highest possible degree for professionals in the wine and service industry. A candidate must past three levels of examinations offered by the Court of Master Sommeliers: the introductory sommelier course, the advanced course, and the master sommelier diploma exams. When a candidate has successfully passed all three levels, he or she earns the Master Sommelier diploma and can be referred to as a Master Sommelier. The courses focus on the areas needed for superior beverage department management, which include tasting, theory, and practical and dining room application. The courses also include spirits, beers, and cigars, as well as global wine knowledge. Only 74 sommeliers in the United States have earned the title Master Sommelier, 13 of whom are women.

Pitfalls

All restaurant service jobs can be enormously high pressure and high stress. When the house is full, the sommelier may have to manage quite a number of tables. Customers can sometimes be difficult but a sommelier must handle all kinds of problems with aplomb. Fine restaurants typically maintain long dining hours; many sommeliers work evenings, weekends, and holidays.

Perks

Top sommeliers are highly sought after and can command excellent salaries, benefits, and respect—from the owner and the chef on down. Usually, sommeliers truly love fine wines and think of their careers not just as a job, but as a way of life.

Get a Jump on the Job

You can't serve wine until you're at least 18 (21 in some states)—but you can certainly start learning the restaurant business in high school, as a waitperson or bus person at a local restaurant. If you're still in high school, it might be easier to get a job at a restaurant without a liquor license (if you're under age, you won't even be able to touch an empty wine glass on a table.) Move on to better restaurants and watch and learn from the sommelier. Let the person know you're interested in wines and hoping to learn more. Finally, read all you can about growing, producing, and tasting fine wines.

SUSHI CHEF

OVERVIEW

It may be an acquired taste, those little rolls of raw seafood and vegetables, but the demands for Japanese sushi continue to increase. And while almost anyone can buy a book and some equipment and start making California rolls, preparing sushi in the style of a Japanese sushi chef requires careful training and a lot of practice.

Sushi making can be traced back to the seventh century, when fish and rice were pressed together as a means of preserving the fish. It's evolved over the centuries into an art form, in which rare and delicate ingredients are used to make healthful, attractive, and delicious bites of food.

In the past, a traditional Japanese sushi chef would train for at least 10 years before he'd be recognized as an *itamae-san* ("sushi chef" in Japanese). Today, however, the demand for sushi chefs is great and the training time has been significantly shortened.

With sushi showing up everywhere from hip, urban sushi bars to small-town grocery store coolers, there are many types of jobs for a sushi chef. You might work behind the scenes, making sushi to be packaged and sold in a store or as part of a restaurant buffet. Or you might toil in a restaurant or sushi bar, making sushi to order for customers.

Regardless of where you work, you'll need to have a lot of knowledge about different types of sushi, the ingredients and methods used to prepare it, the tools necessary for preparation, and the safety concerns associated with making and

AT A GLANCE

Salary Range

An average sushi chef working behind the scenes is likely to earn between $9 and $12 an hour. A good sushi chef working in a sushi bar or restaurant can expect to earn anywhere between $31,000 and $70,000 a year. In a resort city, such as Las Vegas, high-profile sushi chefs can earn as much as $120,000 a year. Salaries will vary, depending on experience and where you're working.

Education/Experience

You can learn to make sushi on your own, but you'll have a real advantage if you complete courses at a specialized sushi school and get certified as a sushi chef. At the very least, you should be trained in food safety and sanitation.

Personal Attributes

A sushi chef should be well trained and disciplined, and able to concentrate intently on the task at hand. Remember that you'll be using extremely sharp knives. However, it also helps to have an outgoing personality and be able to relate well to others, because sushi chefs typically have a lot of interaction with customers. You must also have good personal hygiene and be able to stand for long periods of time.

Requirements

Some employers may require you to have completed an apprenticeship with an experienced sushi chef. Others will require that you have a culinary background.

Outlook

As Americans become better acquainted with sushi and other Japanese foods, the demand for sushi chefs is high.

eating some types of sushi using raw ingredients. While not all sushi contains raw fish (sushi actually refers to the vinegared

Solomon Zamora, sushi chef

Solomon Zamora has more than 20 years of experience in the hotel and restaurant industry, but not all of that time was spent making sushi. "I started in the lowest position in the kitchen and worked my way up through almost every job," Zamora says. "I worked as a dishwasher, kitchen helper, pantry chef, assistant chef, and many other jobs, and I think that was a very good way to learn what I needed to know in order to be a good sushi chef."

Starting at the bottom and learning a variety of restaurant-related jobs—a practice that sometimes is referred to as "start from scratch and eat dust," according to Zamora, provided him with excellent training, and a lot of patience for all types of work. "I'm proud that I am very disciplined in my work," he says. "That came from experiencing most all of the different positions."

Zamora's skill as a sushi chef has landed him jobs in restaurants in five different American states and 10 different countries. There is nothing about the job, he says, that he doesn't enjoy.

"I love being a sushi chef. I have no regrets at all that this is the path I've taken," he says.

The best part of being a sushi chef is that you have the opportunity to make a lot of friends, Zamora says. Working in the front of a restaurant allows you to meet new people all the time and to spend time with those you've met previously. Because you're in the public eye, Zamora explains, it's very important to keep up with current events so that you can talk to people who come to the restaurant for sushi.

"You need to know what's going on in the community and around the world," Zamora says. "You're in direct contact with the guests and you've got to be able to interact with them."

Another important role of a sushi chef is keeping track of supplies and ingredients, he says. You've got to know what ingredients are likely to be available at any given time, and the best places to buy what you need. You need to be aware of costs, availability, and how likely you are to use all the ingredients purchased. Some ingredients used in making sushi are very expensive, and a sushi chef who repeatedly orders supplies that end up being wasted will not remain in good standing with restaurant management.

Zamora says that he spends considerable time each day figuring out what type of sushi to make and what ingredients he'll need to make it, taking into consideration seasonal availability and freshness. Zamora, who has a degree in business administration, has always been interested in restaurant work, but he had thought he might work in restaurants on the business side. Instead, he found himself drawn to food preparation.

His accounting degree is still relevant, he says, but it was the hands-on work in restaurants and hotels that really taught him the business. He learned to make sushi from other sushi chefs, particularly one—who he calls his *sensei*, or teacher. "I believe that experience and hands-on learning are the best teachers and worth more than a diploma from any culinary school or sushi school," Zamora says.

Someone who trains or learns from experience to make sushi, and who performs the job well is likely to have no trouble finding work. "My sensei always told me that as long as there are people eating, I would be able to find a job," Zamora says.

Many people, including Zamora, believe the demand for sushi chefs will continue to grow as people become increasingly aware of the food. "Japanese cooking, including sushi, is a very healthy way to eat," Zamora says. "Japanese cuisine is getting more famous all the time and will continue to for generations to come."

rice used in the finished product), sushi with raw fish must be handled very carefully. Only the freshest fish can be used.

As sushi becomes more widely known and popular in the United States, sushi schools are opening to provide training for would-be chefs. Some of the better-known schools are the California Sushi Academy in Venice, the Sushi Chef Institute in Los Angeles, and the Osaka Sushi Chef School in Scottsdale, Arizona. Training programs range from several months to a couple of years.

Preparing sushi at a sushi bar is as much about presentation as culinary skills. Every sushi chef has his or her own style, but customers generally expect to be entertained as well as fed. A really good sushi chef attracts a following of customers who will wait for a seat at the bar, if necessary.

Pitfalls

Getting to be a really top-notch sushi chef requires years of learning and practice. You may have to be willing to work in lower-paying, lower-profile jobs until you've acquired the skills necessary to be a sushi chef at a top-rate restaurant or sushi bar.

Perks

There's a certain amount of flair needed to prepare sushi in front of customers, who appreciate a little drama along with their Futomaki rolls. If you enjoy entertaining and being the center of attention, and you love to prepare food, this job could be a winner.

Get a Jump on the Job

You can read books and buy recorded TV demonstrations and lessons on sushi making. Keep an eye out for classes in your area—a seafood store or restaurant will sometimes offer a sushi-making course. If there's a sushi bar or restaurant near you, go watch the chef. If the chef seems approachable, share your interest in learning to be a sushi chef and ask if it's okay if you just watch for a while. (This will work better when the restaurant is not overly crowded.) Once you've gained experience in making sushi, look for a master sushi chef for whom you might apprentice.

TEST KITCHEN CHEF

OVERVIEW

Whether you're eating a Big Mac, a frozen dinner, a school lunch meal, a soda, or an ice cream bar, most of what you eat and drink has been developed in a test kitchen. There are all kinds of test kitchens. Food manufacturing companies such as General Mills, Kraft, and Nestle have test kitchens to develop new products. Large food distributors, such as SYSCO, have test kitchens. So do large catering firms, some colleges and universities, food magazines, beverage companies, and restaurant chains. *Consumer Reports,* the magazine that rates everything from cars to baby strollers, has a test kitchen, as does famous TV chef Emeril Lagasse.

Consumers—from tots to the elderly—are getting more demanding all the time. We want to have access to foods that reflect the latest trends, taste great, look appealing, and are easy to eat. It takes constant effort for food providers to keep up with customer demands, and they rely heavily on test kitchen chefs to help them do so.

Take a look at the items on the shelves the next time you're in your local grocery store. Chances are you'll see something new. Or, you'll notice a product with a label that says something like, "Improved Flavor." Test kitchen chefs work both to develop new food products and to improve existing ones. Think of all the new soda flavors that have emerged in recent years: Colas are now flavored with cherry, lemon, lime,

AT A GLANCE

Salary Range

An experienced chef working in a test kitchen can expect to earn between $40,000 and $70,000 a year, depending on the location, type of test kitchen, and the employer.

Education/Experience

Educational requirements for test kitchen chefs vary, depending on the type of job situation you plan to pursue. Many, but not all, test kitchen chefs have completed culinary arts programs at recognized culinary schools. Some, however, enter the field from areas such as food service education or food science. In any case, you're likely to benefit from some formalized education, either a four-year college degree in a culinary, food service, or nutritional-related field, or completion of a culinary arts program.

Personal Attributes

While being a chef in a test kitchen isn't nearly as stressful as the job of a restaurant chef, you should have the ability to withstand some pressure, because food testing has to be very exact. Obviously, you should have a strong interest in food and enjoy cooking. You must have good hygiene, patience to try recipes over and over until they are perfected, and the ability to work with other people. As with many jobs, a good sense of humor is also useful.

Requirements

Requirements vary, depending on the employer. Many employers will require pre-employment physicals and medical background checks.

Outlook

Good. Americans are eating more and more meals away from home, putting a demand on restaurants and food service operations. This trend means there will be an increasing need for test kitchen chefs as well as restaurant chefs and cooks.

Stanton Lyons, test kitchen chef

Stanton Lyons spent 12 years working as a restaurant chef, and for part of that time he has owned a restaurant in Austin, Texas. Moving from restaurant work into a test kitchen was a big change for Lyons, but he finds the experience to be interesting and rewarding. He also enjoys the less stressful atmosphere of the test kitchen. "I was working 90 hours a week and it was incredibly stressful," Lyons says. "I was just so burnt out as a chef, I knew I had to do something different."

He now works for a major food service provider, creating recipes to be used in schools with which the company contracts to provide lunch services. Lyons works as a part of a team that includes graphic designers, dieticians, and concept developers to come up with new ideas for school lunches. Between them, they not only create recipes and test new foods, but works together to create total dining concepts, such as a dining area with lounge-type furniture, attractive food packaging, and, of course, meals that kids love.

Because kids recently have expressed a preference for Asian-style foods, he came up with the concept of a Chinese-to-go meal. The meal is vegetable fried rice, served in a specially designed box. Garnishes and protein toppings (such as chicken) are provided separately, giving students a choice of whether or not to add them to the rice. The Chinese-to-go meal meets nutritional guidelines and is a hit with students.

Developing that and other meals doesn't just happen, however, Lyons says. It requires concentration, careful planning, and a lot of attention to detail. "I can't just cook something, like I would have when I was working online," he says. "I have to figure out and record exactly how much of every ingredient I use, and exactly how the food is prepared. It can get tedious."

A test kitchen chef has to be a combination of a chef and a scientist, Lyons says. "Our test kitchen is almost like a laboratory."

and vanilla. Fast food restaurants come up with enticing new salads or towering new sandwiches. While these products seem to appear out of nowhere, you can bet that they've been painstakingly developed and tested before they appear on the supermarket shelves.

Of course, test kitchen chefs don't spend all of their time in the kitchen. They must research recipes and ingredients, conduct cost analysis, check for availability of ingredients, and perform many other tasks relating to the development of food products.

Pitfalls

Working in a test kitchen requires concentration and the ability to be exacting. The best jobs for test kitchen chefs can be very competitive, and you may have to be willing to relocate to get the one you want.

Perks

If you love food, being a test kitchen chef puts you in the thick of things. In addition to actually cooking, test kitchen chefs predict and study food trends, work with manufacturers and suppliers, conduct surveys and taste tests to see what tastes consumers like the most, and delve into all sorts of food-related issues and developments.

Get a Jump on the Job

Read everything you can about cooking and food development. Learn where the food you eat comes from. If your ice cream bar is a Nestle product, for instance, check out the Nestle Web site and find out everything you can about its operations. This will help you to understand what's involved with getting a product into the grocery store freezer. When you're old enough, get a job in a restaurant and make it clear that you're interested in cooking. Cook at home and experiment with recipes or try to come up with your own recipes. You can also watch the popular public television show *America's Test Kitchen,* where chefs test equipment and ingredients as they prepare various dishes.

WINEMAKER (ENOLOGIST)

OVERVIEW

The warm summer sun beats down on long rows of grapevines, with bunches of glistening fruit perfuming the air with a haunting odor. This bucolic scene is the bailiwick of the enologist—the wine producer—whose job takes him or her out into the fields to check on the vines to the cellars where the bottles are gently aging in racks carefully calibrated by temperature.

The practice of cultivating grapes for wine has been carried on for thousands of years, but it's only been since the early 20th century that governments around the world felt the urge to ensure wine's authenticity by enacting a variety of laws governing its production. For example, only wine from the French region of Champagne may be called *champagne*.

As the best European wines become increasingly expensive, many Americans have turned to their own home-grown products—principally from California, but also grown in Washington, New York, and Pennsylvania. However, every wine-growing region in the United States has different microclimates suited to the cultivation of specific varietals. Most U.S. wineries are small, family- or individually owned businesses, and produce from 3,000 to 10,000 cases per year. Anything more and you're leaving boutique territory and venturing into the mass-market realm.

AT A GLANCE

Salary Range

$45,000 to $65,000 for beginning wine producer; more experienced wine growers can earn upwards of $100,000.

Education/Experience

While experience counts for a lot, these days many winemakers also have a B.S. or M.S. in enology or fermentation science.

Personal Attributes

To be good at this job, you'll need a crafty nose with an excellent sense of smell and taste.

Requirements

Producing excellent wine is an incredibly complex job, and the more you understand about biology and chemistry of wines, the better.

Outlook

Excellent. Well-trained, knowledgeable wine makers are in demand and should continue to be able to find jobs as the popularity of American wines soar.

Winemakers plan, supervise and coordinate the production of wine from selected varieties of grapes, tending to the grape harvest and winemaking. A winemaker works with viticulturists who manage planting programs, and who cultivate and produce the grapes. The winemaker also conducts various laboratory tests to check on the progress of grapes, making sure of their quality and figuring out the best time for harvest. It is the winemaker who decides how the grape should be crushed, pressed, and processed to make the most of the freshly crushed grapes' scents, textures, and flavors. Winemakers also organize the settling of juice and the fermentation of grape material, direct the filtering of wine to remove remaining solids, conduct more lab tests, and monitor the quality of the wine as it's filtered into casks or tanks for storage and maturation. All of this has an influence on the eventual style and flavor of a wine.

Once the wine has matured, the winemaker prepares to bottle the wine, making sure that quality is maintained as the wine is bottled. In addition, a winemaker also must deal with personnel issues and the business end of wine production. They supervise cellar personnel who produce the wine and supervise the maintenance of the vineyard and winery during the off-season. They also spend time with sales and marketing staff to handle publicity of the wine production, with details on wine types, styles, and qualities, and may conduct technical in-service training for cellar staff.

A part of getting good publicity about your wines and the winery involves opening up the place to the public. Many winemakers give guided tours of the winery and vineyards, conduct tastings for the public, and advise visitors about various aspects of wine. Since most wineries and vineyards are located in rural, beautiful parts of the country, many winemakers make the most of the location and also offer special tasting events, public classes, and other events such as musical or dramatic evenings paired with wine.

Scientific knowledge also plays an increasingly important role in winemaking, and some winemakers specialize in the research and development of wine.

Winemakers working in large wineries are in charge of the technical side of the business, whereas those who work in smaller companies may be responsible for the whole winemaking process, from the growing of the grapes to the bottling and marketing of the finished wine. Owners may also be winemakers and enjoy involving themselves in every aspect of the process.

In the constantly changing wine marketplace, future winemakers need to learn about everything, including emerging varietals, new classics, and the latest techniques and ideas about growing grapes.

Some schools offer a bachelor's degree in viticulture or enology, along with a certificate of special study in enology; a few also offer a master of science in viticulture and enology. As part of the curriculum at California State University, Fresno (the only university in North America licensed to produce, bottle, and sell wine commercially), students take two classes in wine production, and the commercial license to produce and sell wine is an important part of enology studies. Some colleges offer programs in viticulture and enology through their horticulture programs, which typically provide lots of information about small fruits and viticulture, the biochemistry of fruit and wine, and information about vineyard management and winery systems. You'll also learn about microbiology and wine processing, regulatory issues and laws, and wine analysis. Some states offer two-year certification courses through the extension service.

If you're thinking about getting into winemaking, you'll need to figure out if you want to cultivate your own grapes, or just own a wine-making facility, buying your grapes from others. If your family doesn't already own a vineyard, coming up with the cash to buy one can be tough. In the Napa

Eric Miller, winemaker

For winemaker Eric Miller, growing wine is first and foremost a sensual experience. "I have a hedonistic interest in wine," he says. "I love the smells and flavors—they drive me crazy." In fact, it's so important to him to see the grapes and enjoy the fragrance that he spends a lot of time out in the vineyards. To him, the vision of winemaker is really more of a wine grower. "I don't see it as a manufacturing job," he explains. "I see it as working with something that's growing, to bring out the most desirable character of the fruit."

As co-owner of Chaddsford Winery along with his brother Lee, Miller and his family work with their 30-acre vineyard—but he also works closely with his vineyard manager to buy grapes from growers working another 300 acres throughout southeastern Pennsylvania. "I go out into the vineyards and I work with the growers," he says. "I'm the only winery in Pennsylvania who does that."

Miller and his brother have been involved in the growth and development of the premium wine industry since the early 1970s. Together they have more than 50 years of experience in winemaking and marketing, and their experience shows not only in their wines, but in the relaxed and friendly atmosphere at the winery.

At each turn of the season, the vine is in a different state, and Miller wants to be there to check out any new developments. He evaluates the vines, understands where the vines should be in each stage of development, and makes recommendations or takes advice. "I'll go all the way to site preparation," he says. "Sometimes I buy the vines myself I select the rootstock, work on spray materials, what size the crop should be, the design of the trellising system."

He works with about 15 different grapes in three different species of grapevines: *labrusca* (a native American species, including Concord and Niagara grapes), *vinifera* (Chardonnay, cabernet, pinot noir), and a third interspecific hybrid. "I go into the field, [and] I make some of my decisions based on the taste of the grape. We also have a sophisticated analysis of grapes and their composition. It starts going through an evolution as it goes through fermentation. If I use a certain yeast type it affects the flavor; if I age it in a barrel it actually absorbs the flavor of the wood; there are a lot of things that affect a wine's smell and flavor. I've been working with those now that I know more about what I'm doing, but I'm still not in control. It's something I like, as much as it's frustrating. It's very complex. Since we're not manufacturing wine and making five-dollar bottles of wine, I hope we're a craft winery. We're interested in that complexity.

"In small wineries you can do it all," Miller says. "In large wineries, it does get departmentalized, where you have the growing side and the seller side."

Miller enjoys just about everything having to do with winemaking—except the number-crunching. "I don't enjoy keeping the books, the numbers part of things," he admits. "But I have to do it."

His advice to young, up-and-coming wine growers and producers? "Please, please, please do it!" he says. "We need the talent and energy here in the East—we are desperately short of trained winemaking talent. We don't need any more amateurs, who go through and learn the discipline. We need people who understand the biology of winemaking."

Miller recommends two schools—Roseworthy in Australia, and the University of California/ Davis. Although you also can study enology in a few eastern universities, the area's varied climate—cool in the north, warm in the continental coast—makes it more difficult. "The enology

(continues)

(continued)

departments now are in Canada and upstate New York—but that's not our climate [in southern Pennsylvania]," Miller explains.

Like many other wineries, Chaddsford is open to the public and offers tastings seven days a week. "I'm really eager to do that," Miller says. "If people don't taste it, they don't really know what we're doing." With that understanding, Miller and his brother decided to run a small class for "weekend winemakers" to more fully explore the process. During this program, the class goes into the vineyard in the morning to learn where it's been, where it is now, and where it's going, and then comes into the winery to talk about the previous vintage—where it is, where it's been, and where it's going.

Acknowledged as Pennsylvania's largest and most recognized winery, Chaddsford has achieved a national reputation for producing world-class but reasonably-priced European style wines from light to rich and earthy. Open year-round for tours, tastings and sales, the Chaddsford Winery is perhaps best known for their chardonnay, but Chaddsford wines have been highly rated in recent reviews in *Food & Wine, Bon Appétit, Wine Enthusiast,* and *Wine Spectator.* Many of their wines, including their merlot, cabernet sauvignon, pinot noir, and chardonnay, have won awards in international wine competitions.

Miller spent a lot of his childhood in Europe, with access to the classic French wines at an early age. The family eventually returned a few years later to Benmarl Vineyards, their old fruit farm in the Hudson Valley, where his mother's Italian family placed great importance on celebration and food: Weddings, graduations, funerals, and ordinations were prefaced by months of cooking.

"Combine these two backgrounds and you have my childhood household," Miller explains. "Dinner was an event, not a meal, and it happened every night. The wine cellar was vast ... and we all had wine with dinner as soon as we were old enough to show an interest." Miller and his brothers could earn spare change at the table if they accepted their dad's nightly challenges to "name that wine."

"I taste wine a lot at the winery, but I never drink it," he says. "I always spit it out. At the end of the day, my reward is that I get to drink wine and pair it with food. That's marvelous! Things happen when you put the two together—one and one is three, because drinking wine with food creates these new flavors that you didn't even know were there."

Valley of California, for example, an acre of prime vineyard goes for about $64,000 to $102,000, not including the extra $15,000 to $20,000 to plant, maintain, and harvest that acre. Moreover, starting from scratch with a boutique vineyard means you won't have any wine to sell for the first five years (three for the vines to bear fruit, and two to age your wine).

If you don't have that kind of capital to invest in starting an average boutique vineyard from the ground up, you might want to consider buying grapes from other growers and making wine from those. That way, you'll knock three years off the time it would take to get your brand to market, although if you're making red wine, you'll still need to cellar the wine for two years.

Pitfalls

Producing quality wines year after year takes expertise in microbiology, agronomy, marketing, enology, and machine repair—or the time and money to hire experts. Winemaking is hard work and requires total determination and dedication. Keep in mind that the market for premium wines is extremely volatile. Sales may plummet due to numerous uncontrollable variables such as poor weather, disease, infestation, or the economy.

Perks

For those who truly love wine and the outdoors, producing boutique wines is as much a beloved lifestyle as a career. There is tremendous enjoyment in making the complex, variable beverage out of grapes in your own vineyard.

Get a Jump on the Job

Even a novice can appreciate a glass of wine, because wine and food are part of daily life. But if you're truly interested in learning more about producing wine and growing grapes, you can start by learning about the chemistry of winemaking. One way to do this is to subscribe to wine newsletters such as *Wine Spectator* or *Wine Advocate*. Research what's involved in winemaking: The University of California at Davis has a world-renowned department of viticulture and enology (http://wineserver.ucdavis.edu) offering programs in all aspects of the business. If you think you might be interested in a career producing wines, check out their Web site, learning about the various vintages and types of grapes. Consider taking a wine-tasting class, which may be offered at a nearby specialty wine shop.

Next, you should work toward and earn a degree in enology, chemistry, biochemistry, or biology, if you're truly determined to pursue a career in the wine industry. For those without winery experience, the best way to get into the production end of the industry is to join the harvest season crew (the harvest is also referred to as *crush*), or take a temporary job on the production end (cellar work, bottling, or lab analysis). Although the position may be temporary, it's impressive to have one season under your belt, and it could lead to a permanent job.

APPENDIX A. ASSOCIATIONS, ORGANIZATIONS, AND WEB SITES

BENIHANA CHEF

Asian Chefs Association
3145 Geary Boulevard #112
San Francisco, CA 94118
(415) 531-3599
info@acasf.com
http://www.acasf.com

An association founded in 2002 to provide a forum for Asian chefs and to promote Asian cuisine and cooking styles. The organization sponsors meetings in various cities, schedules roundtable meetings, and presents receptions in honor of celebrity chefs and other events. It also has a goal of supporting and nurturing young chefs, and of supporting cultural and nonprofit organizations within Asian communities.

Benihana Restaurant Chain
8685 Northwest 53 Terrace
Miami, FL 33166
(305) 593-0770
http://www.benihana.com

The first Benihana restaurant opened in 1964 in New York City, and the chain has grown to 69 restaurants nationwide. The chain also has restaurants in Canada, South America, Asia, Europe, and Australia. The company's Web site provides a wealth of information about the restaurant, the people who run it, its history, the cooking style and food served there, and more.

BREWMASTER

Brewers Association
736 Pearl Street
Boulder, CO 80302
(303) 447-0816
http://www.beertown.org

The Brewers Association was established in 2005 by a merger of the Association of Brewers and the Brewers' Association of America. The association's goal is to unify the combined 88-year history of service and to promote and protect the U.S. craft-brewing community's interests.

National Beer Wholesalers Association
1101 King Street, Suite 600
Alexandria, VA 22314-2944
(703) 683-4300
info@nbwa.org
http://www.nbwa.org/public/login.aspx

The National Beer Wholesalers Association (NBWA) was founded in 1938 as a trade association for the nations' beer wholesalers. The purpose of NBWA is to provide leadership which enhances the independent malt beverage wholesale industry; to advocate before government and the public on behalf of its members; to encourage the responsible consumption of beer; and to provide programs and services that will enhance members' efficiency and effectiveness. NBWA and its members are committed to ensuring that the products they provide are enjoyed legally, responsibly and safely by persons of legal drinking age only. Beer wholesalers, most of which are family-owned and -operated, actively promote safety and education programs that help fight drunk driving and illegal underage purchase and consumption.

BUTCHER

National Cattlemen's Beef Association
9110 East Nichols Avenue, Suite 300
Centennial, CO 80112
(303) 694-0305
info@beefusa.org
http://www.beefusa.org

Started in 1898 as the National Live Stock Growers Association, the present organization is the result of three mergers and several reorganizations. The organization supports the livestock industry in various ways, serving as a strong voice. It recently has recruited six of the country's top meat cutters to train butchers nationwide to cut from underutilized beef parts, resulting in what the beef association is calling beef value cuts.

North American Meat Processors Association
1910 Association Drive
Reston, VA 20191
(703) 758-1900
info@namp.com
http://www.namp.com

The North American Meat Processors Association was founded in 1942 to represent the interests of meat processing companies and associates. It provides member services, including printed and online newsletters, educational programs, meetings, and seminars. It also holds an annual convention for members.

BUTTERBALL TURKEY TALK-LINE EXPERT

Butterball FAQs
http://www.butterball.com/en/
m1ain_canvas.jsp?includePage=faqs.
jsp&t=FAQs&s0=faqs&s1=
Helpful Web site with turkey talk-line "top 50 most often asked questions."

CAKE DECORATOR

American Bakers Association
1350 I Street Northwest, Suite 1290
Washington, DC 20005-3000
(202) 789-0300
info@americanbakers.org
http://www.americanbakers.org

The American Bakers Association represents the interests of the baking industry, providing legislative updates and action, surveys concerning issues relevant to the industry, conferences, and other services for members.

The Retailer's Bakery Association
8201 Greensboro Drive, Suite 300
McLean, VA 22102
(703) 610-9035
rba@rbanet.com
http://www.rbanet.com

The Retailer's Bakery Association is a not-for-profit trade organization that includes a variety of bakery businesses, from small, independent bakers to the bakeries of large, supermarket chains. The organization was founded in 1918. It holds an annual convention and trade show, and works to promote industry standards. The Retailer's Bakery Association also works to provide networking opportunities and education for its members.

CHEESE MAKER

Foreign Type Cheesemakers Association
1211 17th Avenue
Monroe, WI 53566
(608) 325-2507
ftcheese@tds.net
http://www.ftcma.com

The Foreign Type Cheesemakers Association is a milk and cheese testing facility, serving dairy farms in Southern Wisconsin and beyond. The association offers a full range of testing services, with a mission of maintaining the highest quality of dairy product.

Wisconsin Center for Dairy Research
Babcock Hall, Suite 240
1605 Linden Drive
Madison, WI 53706
(608) 262-5970
info@cdr.wisc.edu
http://www.cdr.wisc.edu

Located on the campus of the University of Wisconsin, the Wisconsin Center for Dairy Research is recognized as one of the country's leading dairy research centers. The center trains and certifies cheese makers working toward the master cheese maker designation. Programs focus on making cheese, dairy safety and quality, and dairy ingredients. The center publishes a quarterly newsletter and sponsors a yearly industry conference.

CHEF-INNKEEPER

International Association of Culinary Professionals
304 West Liberty Street, Suite 201
Louisville, KY 40202
(502) 581-9786
iacp@hqtrs.com
http://www.iacp.com

A nonprofit association providing continuing education and development for members who are engaged in the areas of culinary education, communication, or in the preparation of food and drink. The worldwide membership of nearly 4,000 encompasses more than 35 countries and is a who's who of the world of food. IACP is a worldwide forum for the lively development and exchange of information, knowledge, and inspiration within the professional food community.

National Bed and Breakfast Association
http://www.nbba.com/

National organization for B&B owners, providing information, marketing and advertising help.

Professional Association of Innkeepers
207 White Horse Pike
Haddon Heights, NJ 08035
(856) 310-1102
http://www.paii.org/

This association offers a variety of programs and services targeting keepers of the inn as well as those aspiring to the innkeeping profession. The group offers information on bed-and-breakfast operations and finance, guest management software, starting inns and B&Bs, staying profitable, tips on marketing, and fostering a caring, knowledgeable and conscientious community of professional innkeepers through education, information, advocacy, business opportunities, and research relating to the innkeeping industry.

Professional Chef's Association
1207 Hawkeye Court
Fort Collins, CO 80525
(970) 223-4004
http://www.professionalchef.com

Professional chef nonprofit association with job search database, information on federal food laws, bookstores, vendors, conferences, links to vendors, recipes, food facts, and more.

CHOCOLATIER

Chocolate Manufacturers Association
8320 Old Courthouse Road, Suite 300
Vienna, VA 22182
(703) 790-5011
http://www.chocolateusa.org

The Chocolate Manufacturers Association of the United States of America (CMA) was organized in 1923. The mission of CMA is to provide industry leadership to promote, protect, and enhance the chocolate industry's interests through legislative and regulatory programs and public relations. Firms engaged in the manufacture and distribution of cocoa and chocolate products as defined in the U.S. Food and Drug Administration regulations are eligible for membership in CMA. Members produce a substantial portion of the cocoa and chocolate products manufactured in the U.S. Since 1947, members of CMA have been the principal contributors to the American Cocoa Research Institute, advancing scientific research and training relating to cocoa and chocolate.

National Confectioners Association
8320 Old Courthouse Road, Suite 300
Vienna, VA 22182
(703) 790-5750
info@CandyUSA.org
http://www.candyusa.org

Founded in 1884 in Chicago by representatives of 69 confectionery manufacturing firms, the National Confectioners Association (NCA) is one of the oldest trade associations in the world. The NCA is the major association representing the entire confection industry, offering education and leadership in manufacturing, technical research, public relations, retailing practices, government relations, and statistical analyses. Members include domestic and international confectionery manufacturers and suppliers to the industry to meet the increasingly complex challenges and problems that have confronted the industry. Today, NCA is the major association representing the entire confection industry, offering education and leadership in manufacturing, technical research, public relations, retailing practices, government relations, and statistical analyses.

World Cocoa Foundation
8320 Old Courthouse Road, Suite 300
Vienna, VA 22182
(703) 790-5012
http://www.worldcocoafoundation.org/

The World Cocoa Foundation is a comprehensive program that "takes science into the field," improving production efficiency, increasing farmer yields, and using cocoa to promote production reforestation of degraded tropical lands—all in a sustainable, environmentally responsible manner.

CIDER MAKER

Michigan Cider Maker's Guild
Bill Erwin, President
Erwin Orchards, Inc.
61475 Silver Lake Road
South Lyon, MI 48178
(248) 437-0150
info@erwinorchards.com
http://www.ciderguild.org

Concerned over national health and safety issues a few years ago regarding the consumption of apple cider, a small group of cider makers founded the Michigan Cider Maker's Guild. The guild has very strict membership standards, limiting participation to cider makers who adhere to strict operating procedures and meet stringent quality standards. More than 20 cider mills throughout the state belong to the guild, which is modeled after the craft guilds of the Middle Ages. Members work together to assure they produce the best cider possible. The guild sponsors a cider tasting contest at its annual meeting in Ann Arbor.

COFFEE PURVEYOR

International Coffee Organization
22 Berners Street
London
W1T 3DD
England
+44 (0)20 7580 8591
info@ico.org
http://www.ico.org

The International Coffee Organization was founded in 1963 to address the economic issues surrounding the growing and selling of coffee. It addresses relations between coffee-producing and coffee-consuming nations, coffee-growing standards, compensation for workers, and other issues related to the growing and selling of coffee.

National Coffee Association of USA, Inc.
15 Maiden Lane, Suite 1405
New York, NY 10038
(212) 766-4007
info@ncausa.org
http://www.ncausa.org

The National Coffee Association of USA was founded in 1911 to represent the coffee industry. It represents the interests of the coffee industry, working to improve the image of the industry and serving as a liaison between the coffee industry and government. It also provides educational benefits for members and services such as health care. The association holds an annual convention.

COOKBOOK AUTHOR

Authors On The Web
http://www.authorsontheweb.com/features/0112-cookbook/0112-cookbook.asp

This site offers an online question-and-answer session with nine well-known chefs, including Sheila Lukens, Steven Raichlen, Joanne Weir, and David Lebovitz. The questions deal with the mechanics of writing a cookbook, as well as the creative aspects. The site also provides short biographies for each chef.

TishBoyle.com
http://tishboyle.com

The Web site of professional cookbook author Tish Boyle includes her background, an overview of the mechanics of writing a cookbook, recipes, descriptions of the books, contact information, and the opportunity for visitors to write questions for her to answer.

DAIRY FARMER

American Society of Farm Managers and Rural Appraisers
950 Cherry Street, Suite 508
Denver, CO 80222
http://www.asfmra.org

This national organization offers support for professionals and provides management, valuation, and consulting services on agricultural and rural assets.

Center for Rural Affairs
PO Box 406
Walthill, NE 68067
http://www.cfra.org

A private, nonprofit organization that works to strengthen small businesses, family farms and ranches, and rural communities.

National FFA Organization
The National FFA Center
PO Box 68690
Indianapolis, IN 46268-0960
http://www.ffa.org

National organization that tries to make a positive difference in the lives of students by developing their potential for premier leadership, personal growth, and career success through agricultural education.

Small Farm Program
U.S. Department of Agriculture
Cooperative State, Research, Education, and Extension Service
Stop 2220
Washington, DC 20250-2220
http://www.usda.gov/oce/smallfarm/

USDA's program to help small farmers get started in a new farm business.

DOG BISCUIT CHEF

Great Dog Bakery
15365 Southwest Beaverton Creek Court
Beaverton, OR 97006
(877) 292-1113
info@greatdogbakery.com
http://www.greatdogbakery.com

Web site of dog biscuit chef Daryl Ostrovsky, who creates homemade all-natural dog treats.

Start Your Own Dog Bakery Business
http://www.mymommybiz.com/ebooks/
bakeryibm.html

An Internet how-to for those interested in becoming a dog biscuit chef.

Three Dog Bakery
1843 North Topping Avenue
Kansas City, MO 64120
(800) 487-3287
threedog@threedog.com
http://www.threedog.com

A dog biscuit bakery with lots of extras. The company offers a dog bakery cookbook, dog accessories, and contributes and offers consumers the chance to donate to several types of dog-related charities, including the Gracie Foundation for neglected and abused dogs, and the "Leave No Pet Behind Ever Again After Katrina 2005" campaign.

FAST FOOD FRANCHISEE

American Franchisee Association
53 West Jackson Boulevard, Suite 1157
Chicago, IL 60604
(312) 431-0545
webmasterafa@franchisee.org
http://www.franchisee.org

The American Franchisee Association is an organization dedicated to improving the franchising industry and protecting the economic interests of its members. It was founded in 1993, and has more than 7,000 individual members who represent more than 30,000 franchised establishments in 60 different industries.

McDonald's Corporation
2111 McDonald's Drive
Oak Brook, IL 60523
(800) 244-6227
http://www.mcdonalds.com

McDonald's has been an American institution since the first restaurant opened in Des Plaines, Illinois in 1955. It is the world's largest foodservice retailer with more than 30,000 restaurants in 119 countries. McDonald's Web site is packed with information about available franchises, franchising requirements, its history, contact information, and more.

FISH PURVEYOR

National Fisheries Institute, Inc.
7918 Jones Branch Drive, Suite 700
McLean, VA 22102
(703) 752-8880
gthomas@nfi.org
http://www.nfi.org

The National Fisheries Institute is a trade association that represents businesses involved in all aspects of the fish and seafood industry. Members include fish farmers, operators of fishing vessels, importers and exporters of seafood, retail store and restaurant operators, and others. The association advocates for the fish and seafood industry, and works to educate the public about the health benefits of eating fish and seafood. Regional and national meetings are scheduled throughout the year.

FLAIR BARTENDER

BarTrix
2546 North Ashland 2F
Chicago, IL 60614
(815) 592-1667
rob@bartrix.com
http://www.bartrix.com

BarTrix is a Web site dedicated to the profession of flair bartending. It lists flair bartending competitions, includes information on where to get flair

bartending equipment, and offers tips on flair bartending.

Flair Bartender's Association
PO Box 190466
Boise, ID 83719
(208) 484-9900
info@barflair.org
http://www.barflair.org

Founded in 1997 as the Flair Bartender's Network, the Flair Bartender's Association (FBA) works to educate the public about flair bartending and provides workshops and training for its members, organizes flair bartending competitions, and provides public relations services for the industry. The motto of the FBA is "Service First, Flair Second, Competition Always." The FBA's Web site includes video clips and photos of flair bartenders, as well as articles about flair bartending, notices of upcoming competitions, and a forum for association members. The FBA has almost 7,000 members in more than 120 countries.

FOOD PACKAGE DESIGNER

American Institute of Graphic Arts
164 Fifth Avenue
New York NY 10010
(212) 807-1990
http://www.aiga.org

AIGA, the professional association for design, is committed to furthering excellence in design as a strategic tool for business. At AIGA professionals can exchange ideas and information, participate in critical analysis and research, and advance education and ethical practice.

Women in Packaging, Inc.
4290 Bells Ferry Road, Suite 106-17

Kennesaw, GA 30144

http://www.womeninpackaging.org

The foremost packaging association for women that provides a forum for packaging education, networking, and mentoring for the personal and professional development of women. It also promotes diversity across all levels and educates the packaging industry about the contributions and potential of qualified women in packaging. The association also helps to eliminate misconceptions, stereotypes, and discrimination against women in the profession.

FOOD SCULPTOR

International Dairy Foods Association
1250 H Street, Northwest
Suite 900
Washington, DC 20005
(202) 737-4332
http://www.idfa.org

IDFA is the dairy foods industry's collective voice in Washington, DC, throughout the country, and in the international arena. Today, IDFA represents more than 500 dairy food manufacturers, marketers, distributors and industry suppliers across the United States and Canada, and in 20 other countries. IDFA is the umbrella organization for three constituent organizations—the Milk Industry Foundation, the National Cheese Institute, and the International Ice Cream Association. Members range from large multinational corporations to single plant operations, and represent more than 85 percent of the total volume of milk, cultured products, cheese, and ice cream and frozen desserts produced in the United States—an estimated $70 billion a year industry.

Jim Victor, Food Sculptor
201 Cedar Grove Road
Conshohocken, PA 19428
(610) 825-1274
http://www.jimvictor.com/

A sculptor, artist, and teacher whose sculptures have appeared in the New York Times, Philadelphia Magazine, Der Spiegel, *and others. Among his many commissions are various food sculptures, including butter sculptures for several state fairs and chocolate sculptures commemorating entertainment personalities.*

FOOD SERVICE MANAGER

Olde Greenfield Inn
595 Greenfield Road
Lancaster, PA 17601
(717) 393-0668
http://www.theoldegreenfieldinn.com

National Food Service Management Institute
The University of Mississippi
6 Jeanette Phillips Drive
PO Drawer 188
University, MS 38677-0188
(800) 321-3054
http://www.nfsmi.org/Links

The mission of the National Food Service Management Institute is to provide information and services that promote the continuous improvement of child nutrition programs.

National Society for Healthcare Food Service Management
355 Lexington Avenue, 17th Floor
New York, NY 10017
(212) 297-2166
info@hfm.org
http://www.hfm.org/

The National Society for Healthcare Foodservice Management (HFM) represents more than 2,000 on-staff foodservice professionals at acute, extended, and long-term care facilities and suppliers in the United States and Canada. Founded in 1988, HFM is the healthcare foodservice industry's leading resource for educational programming, professional development, advocacy, and innovative business practices that increase patient and staff satisfaction, decrease costs, and define successful operation performance.

FOOD STYLIST

American Culinary Federation
180 Center Place Way
St. Augustine, FL 32095
(800) 624-9458
memberservices@acfchefs.net
http://www.acfchefs.org

The ACF is primarily an organization for chefs, but food stylists and other culinary professionals are eligible to join as associate members. Founded in New York City in 1929 by three chefs' associations, the ACF works to educate those in the culinary profession and promote the image of American chefs. It oversees international cooking competitions held in the United States and sanctions domestic competitions. The organization has three publications and offers apprentice programs and education opportunities and online resources for members. The ACF sponsors regional conferences, a yearly convention, and competitive cooking events nationwide. There are different levels of membership, including one for high school students interested in culinary careers.

Association of Stylists and Coordinators
24 Fifth Avenue
New York, NY 10011

Info@stylistsasc.com
http://www.stylistsasc.com

Formed in 1974, the ASC represents stylists in many different fields, including food styling. The not-for-profit group is a resource for photographers, advertising agencies, and art directors who hire its members. Stylists must have at least three years' working experience in order to be considered for membership in the ASC.

International Association of Culinary Professionals
304 West Liberty Street, Suite 201
Louisville, KY 40202
(502) 589-3602
iacp@hqtrs.com
http://www.iac.com/ccp/index.html

With more than 4,000 members from 35 countries around the world, the IACP offers continuing education and development to men and women involved in food preparation and service, and culinary education and communications. The IACP has various levels of membership and holds an annual conference. It also offers international travel and learning opportunities for members and presents yearly awards to top professionals in the culinary field.

GOURMET FOOD BUSINESS OWNER

Gunther's Gourmet Groceries
PO Box 18215
Richmond, VA 23226
(804) 240-1796
chefmike@gunthersgourmet.com
http://www.gunthersgourmet.com/index.asp

International Association of Culinary Professionals
304 West Liberty Street, Suite 201

Louisville, KY 40202
(502) 581-9786
iacp@hqtrs.com
http://www.iacp.com

A nonprofit association providing continuing education and development for members who are engaged in the areas of culinary education, communication, or in the preparation of food and drink. This association offers a special-interest section called "Entrepreneurs," dedicated to small food-related business owners and independent operators sharing information to help gourmet food operators manage their businesses. IACP is a worldwide forum for the lively development and exchange of information, knowledge, and inspiration within the professional food community.

ICE CREAM TASTE TESTER

International Association of Ice Cream Vendors
100 North 20th Street, 4th Floor
Philadelphia, PA 19103-1443
(215) 564-3484
http://www.iaicv.org

IAICV is a company membership association of suppliers, manufacturers, and anyone engaged in the selling or marketing of ice cream novelty products. Services include legislative and regulatory information, legislative representation, industry-related information, member education, and networking through conferencing.

International Dairy Foods Association
1250 H Street, Northwest, Suite 900
Washington, DC 20005
(202) 737-4332
http://www.idfa.org

IDFA is the dairy foods industry's collective voice in Washington, DC,

throughout the country, and in the international arena. Today, IDFA represents more than 500 dairy food manufacturers, marketers, distributors, and industry suppliers across the United States and Canada, and in 20 other countries. IDFA is the umbrella organization for three constituent organizations—the Milk Industry Foundation, the National Cheese Institute, and the International Ice Cream Association. Members range from large multinational corporations to single plant operations, and represent more than 85 percent of the total volume of milk, cultured products, cheese, and ice cream and frozen desserts produced in the United States—an estimated $70 billion a year industry.

ICE SCULPTOR

Ice Alaska
Phillips Field Road
PO Box 83134
Fairbanks, AK 99708
(907) 451-8250
iceart@icealaska.com
http://www.icealaska.com

Ice Alaska is a nonprofit organization formed to promote the art of ice sculpture and to educate the public about ice art. Members of the group interact with ice sculptors in other countries to foster international relationships, and work to promote different cultures in their art. The group also holds a yearly festival called ICE ART.

National Ice Carving Association
PO Box 3593
Oak Brook, IL 60522-3593
(630) 871-8431
nicaexdir@aol.com
http://www.nica.org

A national organization that promotes the art of ice sculpture. NICA has more than 500 members and organizes ice-carving competitions in different parts of North America. The organization has established standardized guidelines for judging ice carvings, and has helped to organize sculptors and educate the public about the art of ice sculpture. The Web site includes a list of ice sculptors, some of whom offer lessons to those wishing to learn the craft.

MOVIE SET CATERER

American Culinary Federation
180 Center Place Way
St. Augustine, FL 32095
(800) 624-9458
http://www.acfchefs.org/acfwhat.html

ACF is a professional nonprofit organization for chefs and cooks. Its principal goal is to promote the professional image of American chefs worldwide through education among culinarians at all levels, from apprentices to the most accomplished certified master chefs. ACF is the largest and most prestigious organization dedicated to professional chefs in the United States, and helps set professional standards for culinary education and career development. Registered with the U.S. Department of Labor, ACF operates the only comprehensive certification program for chefs in the United States.

Behind the Scenes Catering
Catering and Event Management
9932 Mesa Rim Road
San Diego, CA 92121
(858) 638-1400
http://www.btscenes.com

Since 1985, BTS has provided on-site food and convenience services for events including the 1995 America's

Cup Broadcast Compound, the 1996 Republican National Convention Media Compound, the 1997 ESPN Winter/Summer X-Games, the NBC Olympic compounds at the 2000 Sydney Olympic Games, and many other on-location productions.

International Caterers Association
1200 17th Street Northwest
Washington, DC 20036-3097
(888) 604-5844

The International Caterers Association (ICA) is a nonprofit organization dedicated to providing education, mentoring, and service for professional caterers and promoting the profession of catering to clients, industry members, vendors, and the public.

PASTRY CHEF

American Culinary Federation
180 Center Place Way
St. Augustine, FL 32095
(800) 624-9458
http://www.acfchefs.org

A professional, nonprofit organization for chefs and cooks founded in 1929 in New York City by three chefs' organizations: the Société Culinaire Philanthropique, the Vatel Club, and the Chefs Association of America. The principal goal of the founding chefs is still true to ACF today: to promote the professional image of American chefs worldwide through education among culinarians at all levels, from apprentices to the most accomplished certified master chefs.

Association of Pastry Chefs
http://www.associationofpastrychefs.org/

The Association of Pastry Chefs was founded in 1993 by a small group of pastry chefs working in the London area. The original purpose of formation was to provide a network by which like-minded people could meet socially away from the pressures of the industry, which could work against any form of socializing. Membership is only open to pastry chefs, pastry commis, and companies supplying products and services for pastry chefs only.

Professional Chef's Association
1207 Hawkeye Court
Fort Collins, CO 80525
(877) 392-1443
http://www.professionalchef.com/
Professional membership organization offering classes, conventions, a helpful Web site, legal advice, a job hotline, and much more.

PIZZA MAKER

National Association of Pizzeria Operators
908 South Eighth Street, Suite 200
Louisville, KY 40203
(502) 736-9530
webmaster@napo.com
http://www.napo.com

The National Association of Pizzeria Operators is a group of more than 1,100 independent pizza shop owners. The organization works to obtain necessary goods and services at group rates in order to reduce costs for members. It also seeks to build community among pizzeria operators and to maintain high awareness concerning pizza among the public. Members receive a monthly magazine called Pizza Today.

National Restaurant Association
1200 17th Street Northwest
Washington, DC 20036

(202) 331-5900
http://www.restaurant.org
The goal of the National Restaurant Association is to represent, educate, and promote the ever-expanding restaurant industry. It is the leading business association for the industry, with 60,000 member companies representing more than 300,000 restaurants. The association is a powerful lobbying voice for the restaurant industry, and provides relevant statistics and information to members. It also offers networking opportunities and training and workforce development. The National Restaurant Association's educational division, the National Restaurant Association Educational Foundation, provides educational materials, programs, and resources to members.

PRODUCE BUYER

International Fresh-Cut Produce Association
1600 Duke Street, Suite 440
Alexandria, VA 22314
(703) 299-6282
http://www.fresh-cuts.org

The International Fresh-Cut Produce Association was founded in 1987 with the intention of providing knowledge and technical assistance to assure its members could grow, package, and deliver safe and wholesome product. Its approximately 500 members include retail and food service produce buyers, processors, distributors, and support companies to the fresh-cut produce industry. The association offers a weekly, online newsletter called Cutting Edge.

Produce Marketing Association
1500 Casho Mill Road
Newark, DE 19711

(302) 738-7100
info@pma.com
http://www.pma.com

The Produce Marketing Association was founded as a nonprofit agency in 1949 and today has more than 2,400 members. Membership includes those who market vegetables, fresh fruit, and related products, both nationally and internationally. Members represent those in the food service, retail, production, and distribution aspects of the produce industry. Membership benefits include an information center, weekly newsletter, and member discounts on Produce Marketing Association events and services.

RESTAURANT REVIEWER

Association of Food Journalists
http://www.afjonline.com

The Association of Food Journalists, Inc. is an online networking system for food writers, restaurant reviewers, editors, and others involved with food journalism. Membership includes magazine writers, newspaper journalists, broadcast companies, online services, freelance food writers, cookbook authors, and syndicated columnists. It offers members a monthly newsletter, annual writing contests, guidelines for and suggestions concerning different aspects of food journalism, and other benefits.

International Food, Wine & Travel Writers Association
1142 South Diamond Bar Boulevard
#177
Diamond Bar, CA 91765
(877) 439-8929
admin@ifwtwa.org
http://www.ifwtwa.org

The International Food, Wine & Travel Writers Association (IFWTWA) was founded in Paris in 1956 by a group of writers who wished to critique French food, wine, and hotels. Headquarters were moved to California in 1981, and the organization now has more than 300 members, all of whom are required to meet strict membership standards. The IFWTWA offers education, professional development opportunities, and coordinated media trips for members. Membership includes writers, authors, photographers, and broadcasters. The organization publishes a newsletter and an online magazine.

SCHOOL NUTRITIONIST

The National Association of College & University Food Services
1405 South Harrison Road, Suite 305
Manly Miles Building
Michigan State University
East Lansing, MI 48824
(517) 332-2494
http://www.nacufs.org/

The National Association of College & University Food Services (NACUFS) is the trade association for food service professionals at nearly 650 institutions of higher education in the United States, Canada, and abroad. NACUFS provides members with a full range of educational programs, publications, management services, and networking opportunities. In addition to colleges and universities, over 400 industry suppliers are members of the association.

School Nutrition Association
700 South Washington Street, Suite 300
Alexandria, VA 22314
(703) 739-3900

servicecenter@schoolnutrition.org
http://www.schoolnutrition.org

The School Nutrition Association works to improve the availability and quality of school nutrition programs and raise public awareness of the importance of good school nutrition programs. The association provides education and training as well as certification and credentialing programs to its more than 55,000 members. The School Nutrition Association has 52 state affiliates and hundreds of local chapters. Its sister organization, the Child Nutrition Foundation, is a fund-raising vehicle that raises money to support professional development and outreach. The School Nutrition Association sponsors a variety of conferences and meetings throughout the year, has an online news center called School Foodservice News, *and publishes the* Journal of Child Nutrition & Management.

SOMMELIER

American Sommelier Association
580 Broadway, Suite 716
New York, NY 10012
(212) 226-6805
office@americansommelier.org
http://www.americansommelier.com

A nonprofit national organization with local chapters throughout the United States. Depending on their size and location, chapters conduct classes, meetings, organized tastings, and social events supporting wine education and the enjoyment of wine. Chapters are also devoted to improving the level of wine service in their local area.

Court of Master Sommeliers
American Chapter

1200 Jefferson Street
Napa, CA 94559
(707) 255-7667
courtofms@aol.com
http://www.mastersommeliers.org

Organization established to encourage improved standards of beverage knowledge and service in hotels and restaurants. Education is the Court's charter. The Court offers the three-part Master Sommelier course, and is responsible for holding examinations for the Master Sommelier designation.

International Sommelier Guild
363 Lang Boulevard
Grand Island, NY 14072
(866) 412-0464
info@internationalsommelier.com
http://www.internationalsommelier.com

The International Sommelier Guild is the premier wine-knowledge resource center, providing tailored expert teaching and consultation. It brings together the resources of top educators, industry leaders, premier restaurateurs, wine merchants, wineries, and writers.

Sommelier Society of America
PO Box 20080
West Village Station
New York, NY 10014
(212) 679-4190
http://www.sommeliersocietyofamerica.org

The Sommelier Society of America is the nation's oldest wine teaching organization. Founded in 1954, it is devoted to creating a vital wine society for industry professionals and interested consumers. The society offers wine education classes, tastings, and professional consultation services.

SUSHI CHEF

International Association of Culinary Professionals
304 West Liberty Street, Suite 201
Louisville, KY 40202
(502) 589-3602
iacp@hqtrs.com
http://www.iacp.com/ccp/index.html

With more than 4,000 members from 35 countries around the world, the IACP offers continuing education and development to men and women involved in food preparation and service, and culinary education and communications. The not-for-profit organization has various levels of membership and holds an annual conference. It also offers international travel and learning opportunities for members and presents yearly awards to top professionals in the culinary field.

Sushi Chef Institute
927 Deep Valley Drive, Suite 299
Rolling Hills Estate, CA 90274
(310) 544-0863
contact@sushischool.net
http://www.sushischool.net

The Sushi Chef Institute is dedicated to teaching professional and nonprofessional cooks the philosophy, art, and science of sushi making. Special attention is given to sanitation procedures, safe food handling, and restaurant management.

TEST KITCHEN CHEF

American Culinary Federation
180 Center Place Way
St. Augustine, FL 32095
(800) 624-9458
acf@acfchefs.net
http://www.acfchefs.org

The American Culinary Federation serves to promote the image of American chefs of every sort. The not-for-profit organization has regional chapters, holds an annual convention, and sponsors educational opportunities and contests for its members. There is an annual "chef of the year" competition, which members can enter in a variety of categories.

Research Chefs Association
5775 Peachtree-Dunwoody Road, Building G, Suite 500
Atlanta, GA 30342
(404) 252-3663
RCA@kellencompany.com
http://www.culinology.com

The Research Chefs Association is an organization founded to represent food research and development professionals. Its members promote culinology, the combination of culinary arts with the science of food. Members include chefs, food scientists, nutritionists, food developers, and others. The Research Chefs Association works to provide education and certification for members and sponsors regional events.

WINEMAKER (ENOLOGIST)

Chaddsford Winery
632 Baltimore Pike
Chadds Ford, PA 19317
(610) 388-6221
http://www.chaddsford.com/

Chaddsford Winery is a small premium winery in the Brandywine Valley in southeast Pennsylvania.

Sonoma County Grape Growers Association
PO Box 1959
Sebastopol, CA 95473
(707) 829-3963
info@scgga.org
http://www.sonomagrapevine.org/

The Sonoma County Grape Growers Association represents the farmers who grow grapes in Sonoma County. Grower members sell their grape production to wineries that make wine. Like any farmer, Sonoma County grape growers take great pride in their land and the grapes they produce. Here the focus is on quality production because premium wines can only be made from high-quality grapes.

APPENDIX B. ONLINE CAREER RESOURCES

This volume offers a look inside a wide range of unusual and unique careers that might appeal to someone interested in working in the food industry. Although this book highlights general information about each job, it can really only give you a glimpse into these careers. These entries are intended to whet your appetite and provide you with some career options you maybe never knew existed.

Before jumping into any career, you'll want to do more research to make sure that it's really something you want to pursue for the rest of your life. You'll want to learn as much as you can about the careers in which you're interested; that way, as you continue to do research and talk to people in those particular fields, you can ask informed and intelligent questions that will help you make your decisions. You might want to research the education options for learning the skills you'll need to be successful, along with scholarships, work-study programs, and other opportunities to help you finance that education. If you search long enough, you can find just about anything using the Internet, including additional information about the jobs featured in this book.

* **A word about Internet safety:** The Internet is a wonderful resource for networking. Many job and career sites have forums where students can interact with other people interested in and working in that field. Some sites even offer online chats where people can communicate with each other in real time. They provide students and jobseekers opportunities to make connections and maybe even begin to lay the groundwork for future employment.

But as you use these forums and chats remember, anyone could be on the other side of that computer screen, telling you exactly what you want to hear. It's easy to get wrapped up in the excitement of the moment when you're on a forum or in a chat, interacting with people who share your career interests and aspirations. But be cautious about what kind of personal information you make available on the forums and in the chats; never give out your full name, address, or phone number. Above all, never agree to meet with someone you've met online.

SEARCH ENGINES

When looking for information, there are many different search engines that will help you to find out more about these jobs. While you probably already have a favorite search engine, you might want to take some time to check out some of the others we'll show you here. Some have features that might help you find information not located with the others. Several engines will offer suggestions for ways to narrow your results, or related phrases you might want to search along with your search results. This is handy if you're having trouble locating exactly what you want.

It's also a good idea to learn how to use the advanced search features of your favorite search engines. Knowing that might help you to zero in on exactly the information for which you are searching without wasting time looking through pages of irrelevant hits.

As you use the Internet to search information on the perfect career, keep in mind that like anything you find on the Internet, you need to consider the source from which the information comes.

Some of the most popular Internet search engines are:

AllSearchEngines.com
http://www.allsearchengines.com
This search engine index has links to the major search engines along with search engines grouped by topic. The site includes a page with more than 75 career and job search engines at http://www. allsearchengines.com/careerjobs.html.

AlltheWeb
http://www.alltheweb.com

AltaVista
http://www.altavista.com

Ask.com
http://www.ask.com

Dogpile
http://www.dogpile.com

Excite
http://www.excite.com

Google
http://www.google.com

HotBot
http://www.hotbot.com

LookSmart
http://www.looksmart.com

Lycos
http://www.lycos.com

Mamma.com
http://www.mamma.com

MSN Network
http://www.msn.com

My Way
http://www.goto.com

Teoma
http://www.directhit.com

Vivisimo
http://www.vivisimo.com

Yahoo!
http://www.yahoo.com

HELPFUL WEB SITES

The Internet is a wealth of information on careers—everything from the mundane to the outrageous. There are thousands of sites devoted to helping you find the perfect job for your interests, skills, and talents. The sites listed here are some of the most helpful ones that the authors discovered while researching the jobs in this volume. The sites are listed in alphabetical order and are offered for your information. Their inclusion does not imply endorsement by the authors.

All Experts
http://www.allexperts.com
The oldest and largest free Q&A service on the Internet, AllExperts.com has thousands of volunteer experts who can answer your questions on just about anything. You also can read replies to questions asked by other people. Each

expert has an online profile to help you pick someone you think might be best suited to answer your question. Very easy to use, it's a great resource for finding experts who can help to answer your questions.

America's Career InfoNet
http://www.acinet.org

This site has a wealth of information! You can get a feel for the general job market; check out wages and trends in a particular state for different jobs; and learn more about the knowledge, skills, abilities, and tasks for specific careers; and learn about required certifications for specific careers and how to get them. In addition, you can search for more than 5,000 scholarships and financial opportunities to help pay for your education. This site also maintains a huge career resources library with links to nearly 6,500 online resources. For fun, you can take a break and watch one of nearly 450 videos featuring real people at work—everything from able seamen to zoologists!

Backdoor Jobs: Short-Term Job Adventures, Summer Jobs, Volunteer Vacations, Work Abroad and More
http://www.backdoorjobs.com

This is the Web site of the popular book by the same name, now in its third edition. While not as extensive as the book, the site still offers a wealth of information for people looking for short-term opportunities: internships, seasonal jobs, volunteer vacations, and work abroad. Job opportunities are classified into several categories: Adventure Jobs, Camps, Ranches & Resort Jobs, Ski Resort Jobs, Jobs in the Great Outdoors, Nature Lover Jobs, Sustainable Living and Farming Work, Artistic & Learning Adventures, Heart Work, and Opportunities Abroad.

Boston Works—Job Explainer
http://bostonworks.boston.com/globe/job_explainer/archive.html

For nearly 18 months, the Boston Globe ran a weekly series profiling a wide range of careers. Some of the jobs were more traditional, but with a twist, like the veterinarian who makes house calls. Others were very unique and unusual, like the profile of a Superior of Society monk. The profiles discuss an average day, challenges of the job, required training, salary, and more. Each profile gives an up-close, personal look at that particular career. In addition, the Boston Works Web site (http://bostonworks.boston.com/) has a lot of general employment-related information.

Career Planning at About.com
http://careerplanning.about.com

Just like most of the other About.com topics, the career planning area has a wealth of information, together with links to other information on the Web. Among the essentials are career-planning A-to-Z, a career-planning glossary, information on career choices, and a free career-planning class.

Career Voyages
http://www.careervoyages.gov

This "ultimate road trip to career success" is sponsored by the U.S. Department of Labor and the U.S. Department of Education. This site provides specific information in separate sections for students, parents, career changers, and career advisors. The FAQ offers great information about getting started, the high-growth industries, how to find your perfect job, how to make sure you're qualified for the job you want, tips for paying for the training and education you need, and more. Also helpful are the Hot Careers and the Emerging Fields sections.

Dream Jobs
http://www.salary.com/careers/layouthtmls/crel_display_Cat10.html

The staff at Salary.com takes a look at some wild, wacky, outrageous, and totally cool ways to earn a living. The jobs they highlight include pro skateboarder, computer game guru, nose, diplomat, and much more.

Find It! in DOL
http://www.dol.gov/dol/findit.htm

A handy source for finding information at the extensive U.S. Department of Labor Web site. You can Find It! by broad topic category, or by audience, which includes a section for students.

Fine Living: *Radical Sabbatical*
http://www.fineliving.com/fine/episode_archive/0,1663,FINE_1413_14,00.html#Series873

The show Radical Sabbatical on the Fine Living network looks at people willing to take a chance and follow their dreams and passions. The show focuses on individuals between the ages of 20 and 65 who have made the decision to leave successful, lucrative careers to start over, usually in an unconventional career. You can read all about these people and their journeys on the show's Web site.

Free Salary Survey Reports and Cost of Living Reports
http://www.salaryexpert.com

Based on information from a number of sources, Salary Expert will tell you what kind of salary you can expect to make for a certain job in a certain geographic location. Salary Expert has information on hundreds of jobs—everything from

more traditional jobs to some unique, out-of-the-ordinary professions such as acupressurist, blacksmith, denture waxer, taxidermist, and many others. With sections covering schools, crime, community comparison, community explorer, this Web site is filled with helpful info. You might also find the moving center a useful site for those who need to relocate for training or employment.

Fun Jobs
http://www.funjobs.com

Fun Jobs has job listings for adventure, outdoor, and fun jobs at ranches, camps, ski resorts, and more. The job postings have a lot of information about the position, requirements, benefits, and responsibilities so that you know what you are getting into ahead of time. And you can apply online for most of the positions. In addition, the Fun Companies link will let you look up companies in an A to Z listing, or you can search for companies in a specific area or by keyword. The company listings offer you more detailed information about the location, types of jobs available, employment qualifications, and more.

Girls Can Do
http://www.girlscando.com

"Helping Girls Discover Their Life's Passions," this Web site has opportunities, resources, and lots of other cool stuff for girls ages 8 to 18. Visitors can explore sections on Outdoor Adventure, Sports, My Body, The Arts, Sci-Tech, Change the World, and Learn, Earn, and Intern. In addition to reading about women in all sorts of careers, girls can explore a wide range of opportunities and information that will help them grow into strong, intelligent, capable women.

Great Web Sites for Kids
http://www.ala.org/gwstemplate.cfm?section=greatwebsites&template=/cfapps/gws/default.cfm

Great Web Sites for Kids is a collection of more than 700 sites organized into a variety of categories, including animals, sciences, the arts, reference, social sciences, and more. All of the sites included here have been approved by a committee made up of professional librarians and educators.

Hot Jobs: Career Tools Home
http://www.hotjobs.com/htdocs/tools/index-us.html

While the jobs listed at Hot Jobs are more on the traditional side, the Career Tools area has a lot of great resources for anyone looking for a job. You'll find information about how to write a resume and a cover letter, how to put together a career portfolio, interviewing tips, links to career assessments, and much more.

Job Descriptions & Job Details
http://www.job-descriptions.org

Search for descriptions and details for more than 13,000 jobs at this site. You can search for jobs by category or by industry. You'd probably be hard pressed to find a job that isn't listed here, and you'll probably find lots of jobs you never imagined existed. The descriptions and details are short, but it's interesting and fun, and might lead you to the career of your dreams.

Job Hunter's Bible
http://www.jobhuntersbible.com

This site is the official online supplement to the book What Color Is Your Parachute? A Practical Manual for Job-Hunters and Career-Changers, *and is a great source of information with lots of informative, helpful articles and links to many more resources.*

Job Profiles
http://www.jobprofiles.org

This site offers a collection of profiles in which experienced workers share rewards of their job, stressful parts of the job, basic skills needed and challenges of the future, together with advice on entering the field. The careers include everything from baseball ticket manager to pastry chef and much, much more. The hundreds of profiles are arranged by broad category. While most of the profiles are easy to read, you can check out the "how to browse JobProfiles.org" section (http://www.jobprofiles.org/jphowto.htm) if you have any problems.

Major Job Web Sites at Careers.org
http://www.careers.org/topic/01_jobs_10.html

This page at the Careers.org Web site has links for more than 40 of the Web's major job-related Web sites. While you're there, check out the numerous links to additional information.

Monster Jobs
http://www.monster.com

Monster.com is one of the largest, and probably best known, job resource sites on the Internet. It's really one-stop shopping for almost any job-related subject that you can imagine: Find a new job, network, update your resume, improve your skills, plan a job change or relocation, and so much more! Of special interest are the Monster: Cool Careers (http://change.monster.com/archives/coolcareers) and Monster: Job Profiles (http://jobprofiles.monster.com) sections, where you can read about some really neat careers. The short profiles also include links to additional information.

*The Monster: Career Advice section
(http://content.monster.com) has resume
and interviewing advice, message boards
where you can network, relocation tools
and advice, and more.*

Occupational Outlook Handbook
http://www.bls.gov/oco

*Published by the U.S. Department of
Labor's Bureau of Labor Statistics,
the Occupational Outlook Handbook
(sometimes referred to as the OOH)
is the premiere source of career
information. The book is updated every
two years, so you can be assured that
the information you are using to help
make your decisions is current. The
online version is very easy to use; you can
search for a specific occupation, browse
though a group of related occupations, or
look through an alphabetical listing of all
the jobs included in the volume. Each of
the entries highlights the general nature
of the job, working conditions, training
and other qualifications, job outlook,
average earning, related occupations, and
sources of additional information. Each
entry covers several pages and is a terrific
source to get some great information
about a huge variety of jobs.*

Online Cooking School
http://the-art-institute-online.com/
index.jsp

*You may love to cook, but you can't
learn how to bake an Alaska or create
a mousse online. Once you have an
associate's degree, however, and you're
looking to get a bachelor's degree, online
culinary schools are a great option. This
online cooking school offers a bachelor's
degree completion program in culinary
management where you can study human
resource management, hospitality law,
restaurant-related business, and more.*

The Riley Guide: Employment Opportunities and Job Resources on the Internet
http://www.rileyguide.com

*The Riley Guide is an amazing collection
of job and career resources. Unless
you're looking for something specific,
one of the best ways to maneuver
around the site is with the A-to-Z Index.
You can find everything from links to
careers in enology to information about
researching companies and employers.
The Riley Guide is a great place to find
just about anything you're looking for,
and probably lots of things you never
dreamed you wanted to know! But be
forewarned—it's easy to get lost in the
A-to-Z Index, because it's filled with so
many interesting things.*

SommelierJobs.com
http://www.sommelierjobs.com

*This is the one place on the Web where
you can find more than 1,000 certified
sommeliers: floor sommeliers, wine
directors, cellarmasters, restaurant
managers, F&B directors, lounge
managers, beverage managers &
maitre d's, winery sales managers, and
even chefs. All with formal sommelier
credentials ranging from certificate, to
advanced master sommelier.*

USA TODAY Career Focus
http://www.usatoday.com/careers/dream/
dreamarc.htm

*USA TODAY offers its "dream job"
series on this Web site. In these interview
profiles, people discuss how they got
their dream job, what they enjoy the
most about it, describe an average
day, their education backgrounds,
sacrifices they had to make for their
jobs, and more. They also share words
of advice for anyone hoping to follow*

in their footsteps. Most of the articles also feature links where you can find more information. The USATODAY. com Job Center (http://www.usatoday. com/money/jobcenter/front.htm) also has links to lots of resources and additional information.

CAREER TESTS AND INVENTORIES

If you have no idea what career is right for you, there are many resources available online that you can use to categorize your interests and steer you in the right direction. While some of the assessments charge a fee, many others are free. You can locate more tests and inventories by entering the following keywords in a search engine: career tests, career inventories, or personality inventories. Some of the most popular assessments available online are:

Campbell Interest and Skill Survey (CISS)
http://www.usnews.com/usnews/edu/careers/ccciss.htm

Career Explorer
http://careerexplorer.net/aptitude.asp

Career Focus 2000 Interest Inventory
http://www.iccweb.com/careerfocus

The Career Interests Game
http://career.missouri.edu/students/explore/thecareerinterestsgame.php

CAREERLINK Inventory
http://www.mpc.edu/cl/cl.htm

The Career Key
http://www.careerkey.org

Career Maze
http://www.careermaze.com/home.asp?licensee=CareerMaze

Career Tests at CareerPlanner.com
http://www.careerplanner.com

FOCUS
http://www.focuscareer.com

Keirsey Temperament Test
http://www.keirsey.com

Motivational Appraisal of Personal Potential (MAPP)
http://www.assessment.com

Myers-Briggs Personality Type
http://www.personalitypathways.com/type_inventory.html

Princeton Review Career Quiz
http://www.princetonreview.com/cte/quiz/default.asp

Skills Profiler
http://www.acinet.org/acinet/skills_home.asp

APPENDIX C. CULINARY SCHOOLS

Although experience is helpful, a culinary degree can really help jump-start your food-related career. Two to four years of solid educational experience can cover what it might take years of work experience to learn. In school you will study under many chefs and gain the benefit of their experience, knowledge, and connections.

When choosing a school, make sure the faculty is qualified. Instructor credentials should include certification by the American Culinary Federation, a college degree, and/ or other relevant industry experience. You may think you already know how to throw eggs and flour together to make a cake, but culinary classes will also teach how to keep your kitchen germ-free, how to handle eggs, cream, and butter, and at what temperatures to properly cook foods to destroy bacteria. You'll also learn the physiology of taste and how sweet, salty, and bitter flavors and textures affect taste buds. Kitchen lessons will teach you how to measure raw ingredients, how to properly handle a knife and kitchen tools, and how to make various foods.

At a restaurant management school, you'll combine managerial theory with practical, hands-on training so that when you graduate, you'll not only know what to do, but how to do it. At restaurant management school, you'll learn important management techniques and basic culinary skills.

At a hotel management college, you'll study all areas of the culinary industry but you'll focus on resorts and hotels, with practical training to help you develop the supervisory skills necessary in the hotel industry.

Many culinary institutes in the United States are associated with the Le Cordon Bleu cooking school, combining classical French techniques with modern American technology. At Cordon Bleu schools, you'll learn the theories behind the skills you'll be developing throughout the course, and you'll get hands-on training to help you develop your own personal skills. Le Cordon Bleu Schools also make sure you'll understand all levels of restaurant operations, including management and leadership theory.

WHAT TO LOOK FOR IN A COOKING SCHOOL

If you're considering a specific culinary institute or cooking school, first check out how many kids are in each class. This is called the student/teacher ratio, and it's a good indication of how much time the teachers will have to spend with each student. Cooking is a physical skill that must be learned, and you need the chance to practice with an instructor.

When visiting a school, talk to faculty, current students, and alumni—not just the admissions staff. Look around you. Does the faculty seem to be in touch with students? Do they have a range of experience, talent, and expertise? Find out how much time they'll actually spend in class. Next, ask about the internships and what you'll be expected to learn. If you know a chef or you're working with restaurant employers, ask them for their opinion about the schools you're considering.

ALABAMA

**The Culinary Institute of Virginia
College**
65 Bagby Drive
Birmingham, AL 35209
(205) 802-1200
http://www.culinard.com/files/page.
cfm?pid=5

ARIZONA

Arizona Culinary Institute
10585 North 114th Street, Suite 401
Scottsdale, AZ 85259
(480) 603-1066
http://www.azculinary.com

Art Institute of Phoenix
2233 West Dunlap Avenue
Phoenix, AZ 85021-2859
(800) 474-2479
http:// www.aipx.edu

Scottsdale Culinary Institute
8100 East Camelback Road
Suite 1001
Scottsdale, AZ 85251
(800) 848-2433
http://www.chefs.edu

CALIFORNIA

The Art Institute of California–Los Angeles
School of Culinary Arts
2900 31st Street
Santa Monica, CA 90405-3035
(310) 752-4700 Ext. 122
http://www.aila.artinstitutes.edu

**The Art Institute of California–
Orange County**
Culinary Arts
3601 Sunflower Avenue

Santa Ana, CA 92704
(888) 549-3055
http://www.aicaoc.artinstitutes.edu

**The Art Institute of California–
San Diego**
7650 Mission Valley Road
San Diego, CA 92108
(858) 598-1208
http://www.aicasd.artinstitutes.edu

California Culinary Academy
625 Polk Street
San Francisco, CA 94102
(800) 229-2433
http://www.baychef.com/

California School of Culinary Arts
Le Cordon Bleu Programs
521 East Green Street
Pasadena, CA 91101
(888) 900-CHEF
http://www.csca.edu

City College of San Francisco
Culinary Arts and Hospitality Studies
Department
50 Phelan Avenue
SW156
San Francisco, CA 94112
(415) 239-3152
http://www.ccsf.edu

Professional Culinary Institute
700 West Hamilton Avenue, Suite 300
Campbell, CA 95008
(888) PCI-LEARN
http://www.pcichef.com

San Diego Culinary Institute
8024 La Mesa Boulevard
La Mesa, CA 91941
(619) 644-2100
info@sdci-inc.com
http://www.sdci-inc.com

Sushi Chef Institute
927 Deep Valley Drive
Suite 299
Rolling Hills Estate, CA 90274
(310) 544-0863
http://www.sushischool.net

CANADA

Culinary Institute of Canada
4 Sydney Street
Charlottetown, Prince Edward Island PE
C1A 1E9
Canada
(902) 894-6805
http://www.hollandc.pe.ca/CIC/

Niagara Culinary Institute
135 Taylor Road, RR #4
Niagara on-the-Lake, ON L0S 1J0
Canada
(905) 641-2252 Ext. 4636
http://niagarac.on.ca/studying/programs/
fulltime/nci_0435/

Northwest Culinary Academy of Vancouver
2725 Main Street
Vancouver, BC V5T 3E9
Canada
(866) 876-2433
http:// www.nwcav.com

Pacific Institute of Culinary Arts
1505 West 2nd Avenue
Vancouver, BC V6H 3Y4
Canada
(800) 416-4040
http://www.picachef.com

COLORADO

The Art Institute of Colorado
School of Culinary Arts
1200 Lincoln Street

Denver, CO 80203
(303) 837-0825
http://cia.aii.edu/programdegrees.
asp?pid=47&dtid=6

Cook Street School of Fine Cooking
Cook Street Food and Wine Career
Program
1937 Market Street
Denver, CO 80202
(303) 308-9300 Ext. 116
http://www.cookstreet.com

Johnson & Wales University
College of Culinary Arts
7150 Montview Boulevard
Denver, CO 80220
(877) 598-3368
http://culinary.jwu.edu/

CONNECTICUT

Center for Culinary Arts
106 Sebethe Drive
Cromwell, CT 06416
(860) 613-3350
http://www.centerforculinaryarts.com/

Center for Culinary Arts
8 Progress Drive
Shelton, CT 06484
(203) 929-0592

Connecticut Culinary Institute
Advanced Culinary Arts Program
230 Farmington Avenue
Farmington, CT 06032
(800) 762-4337
http://www.ctculinary.com/

FLORIDA

The Art Institute of Fort Lauderdale
School of Culinary Arts
1799 Southeast 17th Street Causeway

Fort Lauderdale, FL 33316
(800) 275-7603 Ext. 2149
http://www.aifl.edu/

Capital Culinary Institute of Keiser College
1700 Halstead Boulevard
Building 2
Tallahassee, FL 32309
(877) CHEF-123
http://www.capitalculinaryinstitute.com/

Florida Culinary Institute
2400 Metrocentre Boulevard
West Palm Beach, FL 33407
(561) 842-8324 Ext. 202
http://www.floridaculinary.com

Johnson & Wales University
College of Culinary Arts
1701 Northeast 127th Street
North Miami, FL 33181
(800) BEA-CHEF
http://culinary.jwu.edu/

Le Cordon Bleu College of Culinary Arts
3221 Enterprise Way
Miramar, FL 33025
http://www.miamiculinary.com
(866) 762-2433

GEORGIA

The Art Institute of Atlanta
Culinary Arts Program
6600 Peachtree Dunwoody Road
100 Embassy Row
Atlanta, GA 30328
(800) 275-4242
http://www.aia.artinstitutes.edu

Le Cordon Bleu College of Culinary Arts–Atlanta
1927 Lakeside Parkway
Tucker, GA 30084
http://www.atlantaculinary.com

ILLINOIS

The Cooking and Hospitality Institute of Chicago
361 West Chestnut Street
Chicago, IL 60610-3050
(312) 873-2064
http://www.chic.edu

The Illinois Institute of Art
Culinary Arts
180 North Wabash Avenue
Chicago, IL 60601
(800) 351-3450
http://www.ilic.artinstitutes.edu

Institute of Culinary Arts
401 South State Street
Chicago, IL 60605
(312) 935-6800
http://www.culinaryschools.com/
schools/1221.html

Kendall College
School of Culinary Arts and School of Hotel Management
900 North North Branch Street
Chicago, IL 60622
(877) 588-8860
http://www.kendall.edu

INDIANA

Ivy Tech State College–Central Indiana
Hospitality Administration Program
One West 26th Street
Indianapolis, IN 46208
(317) 921-4516
http://www.ivytech.edu/indianapolis/

KENTUCKY

Sullivan University
National Center for Hospitality Studies
3101 Bardstown Road

Louisville, KY 40205
(502) 456-6505
http://www.sullivan.edu/

LOUISIANA

Louisiana Culinary Institute
5837 Essen Lane
Baton Rouge, LA 70810
(877) 769-8820
http://www.louisianaculinary.com/

MARYLAND

Baltimore International College
School of Culinary Arts
17 Commerce Street
Baltimore, MD 21202-3230
(410) 752-4710 Ext. 120
http://www.bic.edu/

L'Academie de Cuisine
5021 Wilson Lane
Bethesda, MD 20817
(301) 986-9490
classes@lacademie.com
http://www.lacademie.com/index_revert.
html

MASSACHUSETTS

Bunker Hill Community College
Culinary Arts Program
250 New Rutherford Avenue
Boston, MA 02129
(617) 228-2171
http://www.bhcc.mass.edu/

The Cambridge School of Culinary Arts
Professional Chef's Program
2020 Massachusetts Avenue
Cambridge, MA 02140-2104
(617) 354-2020
http://www.cambridgeculinary.com/

International Institute of Culinary Arts
215 Bank Street
Fall River, MA 02720
(508) 675-9305
http://www.iicaculinary.com/

Newbury College
129 Fisher Avenue
Brookline, MA 02445
(617) 730-7007
http://www.newbury.edu/

MICHIGAN

Schoolcraft College
Culinary Arts
18600 Haggerty Road
Livonia, MI 48152-2696
(734) 462-4426
http://www.schoolcraft.edu/

MINNESOTA

The Art Institutes International Minnesota
Culinary Arts
15 South Ninth Street
Minneapolis, MN 55402-3137
(612) 332-3361
http://www.aim.artinstitutes.edu/

Brown College Le Cordon Bleu Culinary Program
1440 Northland Drive
Mendota Heights, MN 55120
(800) 528-4575

Le Cordon Bleu College of Culinary Arts–Minneapolis/ St. Paul
1315 Mendota Heights Road
Mendota Heights, MN 55120
http://www.twincitiesculinary.com/

MISSISSIPPI

Mississippi University for Women
Culinary Arts Institute
1100 College Street
W-1639
Columbus, MS 39701
(662) 241-7472
http://www.muw.edu/

NEVADA

The Art Institute of Las Vegas
2350 Corporate Circle
Henderson, NV 89074
(702) 369-9944
http://www.ailv.artinstitutes.edu/

**Le Cordon Bleu College of
Culinary Arts Las Vegas**
1451 Center Crossing Road
Las Vegas, NV 89144
http://www.lecordonbleuschoolsusa.
com/lasvegas.asp

NEW HAMPSHIRE

**Atlantic Culinary Academy of
McIntosh College**
181 Silver Street
Dover, NH 03820
(877) 628-1222
http://www.atlanticculinary.com/

Southern New Hampshire University
The School of Hospitality, Tourism,
and Culinary Management
2500 North River Road
Manchester, NH 03106-1045
(800) 642-4968
http://www.snhu.edu/

NEW JERSEY

Atlantic Cape Community College
Academy of Culinary Arts

5100 Black Horse Pike
Mays Landing, NJ 08330-2699
(609) 343-5009
http://www.atlantic.edu/

Hudson County Community College
Culinary Arts Institute
161 Newkirk Street
Jersey City, NJ 07306
(201) 714-2193
http://www.hudson.cc.nj.us/

NEW YORK

The Art Institute of New York City
Culinary Arts and Restaurant
Management
75 Varick Street
16th Floor
New York, NY 10013
(212) 226-5500 Ext. 6005
http://ainyc.artinstitutes.edu/

Culinary Institute of America
1946 Campus Drive
Hyde Park, NY 12538-1499
(800) CULINARY
http://www.ciachef.edu/

French Culinary Institute
434 Broadway
7th Floor
New York, NY 10013
(888) FCI-CHEF
http://www.frenchculinary.com

The Institute of Culinary Education
50 West 23rd Street
New York, NY 10010
(212) 847-0711
http://www.iceculinary.com/cookschools

Monroe College
Hospitality Management
2501 Jerome Avenue

Bronx, NY 10468
(718) 933-6700 Ext. 250
http://www.monroecollege.edu/

Natural Gourmet Cookery School
48 West 21st Street, 2nd floor
New York, NY 10010
info@naturalgourmetschool.com
http://www.naturalgourmetschool.com/

New York University
Food Studies and Public Health
35 West 4th Street, 10th Floor
New York, NY 10012-1172
(212) 998-5580
http://education.nyu.edu/nutrition/

Paul Smith's College of Arts and Sciences
Routes 86 and 30
PO Box 265
Paul Smiths, NY 12970
(800) 421-2605
http://www.culinaryschools.com/
schools/75.html

State University of New York College of Agriculture and Technology at Cobleskill
Culinary Arts, Hospitality, and Tourism
Knapp Hall
Cobleskill, NY 12043
(800) 295-8988
http://www.cobleskill.edu/

State University of New York College of Technology at Delhi
Hospitality Management
119 Bush Hall
Main Street
Delhi, NY 13753
(607) 746-4550
http://www.delhi.edu/

NORTH CAROLINA

The Art Institute of Charlotte
Culinary Arts

Three Lake Pointe Plaza
2110 Water Ridge Parkway
Charlotte, NC 28217
(800) 872-4417
http://www.aich.artinstitutes.edu/

Johnson & Wales University
College of Culinary Arts
901 West Trade Street
Charlotte, NC 28202
(980) 598-1100
http://www.jwu.edu/

OKLAHOMA

Culinary Institute of Platt College
2727 West Memorial
Oklahoma City, OK 73134
(405) 749-2433
http://www.plattcollege.org

OREGON

Oregon Coast Culinary Institute
1988 Newmark Avenue
Coos Bay, OR 97420
(877) 895-CHEF
http://www.occi.net/

Western Culinary Institute
1201 Southwest 12th Avenue #100
Portland, OR 97201
(503) 223-2245
http://www.wci.edu/

PENNSYLVANIA

The Art Institute of Philadelphia
Culinary Arts
1622 Chestnut Street
Philadelphia, PA 19103
(800) 275-2474
http://www.aiph.artinstitutes.edu/

The Art Institute of Pittsburgh
420 Boulevard of the Allies
Pittsburgh, PA 15219
(800) 275-2470
http://www.aip.artinstitutes.edu/index2.
asp

Indiana University of Pennsylvania
Academy of Culinary Arts
1010 Winslow Street
Punxsutawney, PA 15767
(800) 438-6424
http://www.iup.edu/

JNA Institute of Culinary Arts
1212 South Broad Street
Philadelphia, PA 19146
(215) 468-8800
http://www.culinaryarts.com/

Mercyhurst College
The Culinary and Wine Institute of
Mercyhurst North East
16 West Division Street
North East, PA 16428
(814) 725-6144
www.mercyhurst.edu/

Pennsylvania College of Technology
School of Hospitality
One College Avenue
Williamsport, PA 17701
(570) 326-3761 Ext. 4671
http://www.pct.edu/

Pennsylvania Culinary Institute
Le Cordon Bleu Culinary Arts
717 Liberty Avenue
Pittsburgh, PA 15222-3500
(800) 432-2433
http://www.pci.edu/

The Restaurant School at Walnut Hill College
School of Hospitality Management/
School of Culinary and Pastry Arts
4207 Walnut Street

Philadelphia, PA 19104
(215) 222-4200 Ext. 3011
http://www.walnuthillcollege.
com/

School of Culinary Arts
West 7th Avenue
York, PA 17404
(800) 840-1004
http://www.yorkchef.com/

York Technical Institute
L'École de Cuisine
Lancaster Campus
3050 Hempland Road
Lancaster, PA 17601
(717) 295-1100
http://chefs.yti.edu/

Yorktowne Business Institute
School of Culinary Arts
West 7th Avenue
York, PA 17404
(800) 840-1004
http://www.ybi.edu/

RHODE ISLAND

Johnson & Wales University
College of Culinary Arts
8 Abbott Park Place
Providence, RI 02903
(800) 342-5598 Ext. 2370
http://www.jwu.edu/prov/

SOUTH CAROLINA

Trident Technical College
Hospitality, Tourism, and
Culinary Arts
PO Box 118067
HT-P
Charleston, SC 29423-8067
(843) 722-5557
http://www.tridenttech.edu/

TEXAS

The Art Institute of Dallas
Culinary Arts
Two North Park East
8080 Park Lane
Suite 100
Dallas, TX 75231
(800) 275-4243
http://www.aid.aii.edu/

The Art Institute of Houston
The School of Culinary Arts
1900 Yorktown
Houston, TX 77056
(800) 275-4244 Ext. 3612
http://www.artinstitutes.edu/
houston/

Culinary Academy of Austin
2823 Hancock Drive
Austin, TX 78731
(512) 451-5743
info@culinaryacademyofaustin.
com
http://www.culinaryacademyof
austin.com/

**Culinary Institute of Alain and
Marie LeNotre**
7070 Allensby
Houston, TX 77022
(713) 692-0077
http://www.lenotre-alain-marie.com

Texas Culinary Academy
11400 Burnet Road
Suite 2100
Austin, TX 78758
(512) 837-2665
http://www.tca.edu/

VERMONT

New England Culinary Institute
250 Main Street
Montpelier, VT 05602
(802) 223-6324
http://www.neci.edu/home

VIRGINIA

The Art Institute of Washington
1820 North Fort Myer Drive
Arlington, VA 22209
(703) 358-9550
http://www.aiw.artinstitutes.edu/

Stratford University
School of Culinary Arts
7777 Leesburg Pike
Suite 100 South
Falls Church, VA 22043
(703) 821-8570
http://www.stratford.edu/

Virginia Intermont College
Culinary Arts Department
1013 Moore Street
Bristol, VA 24201
(276) 466-7850
http://www.vic.edu/index.shtml

WASHINGTON

The Art Institute of Seattle
Culinary Arts Program
2323 Elliott Avenue
Seattle, WA 98121
(206) 448-6600
http://www.ais.edu/

READ MORE ABOUT IT

The following sources and books may help you learn more about careers in the food industry.

GENERAL CAREERS

Boulud, Daniel. *Letters to a Young Chef.* New York: Basic Books, 2003.

Bourdain, Anthony. *Kitchen Confidential: Adventures in the Culinary Underbelly.* New York: Ecco, 2001.

Culbreath, Alice N., and Saundra K. Neal. *Testing the Waters: A Teen's Guide to Career Exploration.* New York: JRC Consulting, 1999.

Culinary Institute of America. *The Professional Chef.* 7th ed. New York: Wiley, 2001.

Davis, Dawn. *If You Can Stand the Heat: Tales from Chefs and Restaurateurs.* New York: Penguin, 1999.

Donovan, Mary. *Careers for Gourmets & Others Who Relish Food.* Chicago: VGM Career Books, 1993.

———. *Opportunities in Culinary Careers.* New York: McGraw-Hill, 2003.

Dornenburg, Andrews. *Becoming a Chef.* New York: Wiley, 2003.

———. *Culinary Artistry.* New York: Wiley, 1996.

Farr, Michael, LaVerne L. Ludden, and Laurence Shatkin. *200 Best Jobs for College Graduates.* Indianapolis, Ind.: Jist Publishing, 2003.

Fogg, Neeta, Paul Harrington, and Thomas Harrington. *College Majors Handbook with Real Career Paths and Payoffs: The Actual Jobs, Earnings, and Trends for Graduates of 60 College Majors.* Indianapolis, Ind.: Jist Publishing, 2004.

Krannich, Ronald L., and Caryl Rae Krannich. *The Best Jobs for the 1990s and into the 21st Century.* Manassas Park, Va.: Impact Publications, 1995.

Mannion, James. *The Everything Alternative Careers Book: Leave the Office Behind and Embark on a New Adventure.* Boston: Adams, 2004.

Masi, Mary. *Culinary Arts Career Starter.* Las Vegas: LearningExpress, 1999.

McGee, Harold. *On Food and Cooking: The Science and Lore of the Kitchen.* New York: Scribner, 2004.

Muir, Jenni. *Cooking School Holidays: In the World's Most Exceptional Places.* New York: Abbeville Press, 2004.

Pepin, Jacques. *The Apprentice: My Life in the Kitchen.* New York: Houghton Mifflin, 2004.

Ruhlman, Michael. *The Soul of a Chef: The Journey Toward Perfection.* New York: Penguin, 2001.

———. *The Making of a Chef: Mastering Heat at the Culinary Institute.* New York: Owl Books, 1999.

Shawguides, Inc. *The Guide to Cooking Schools, 2005: Cooking Schools, Courses, Vacations, Apprenticeships and Wine Programs Throughout the World.* 17th ed. New York: Shaw Guides, 2004.

U.S. Bureau of Labor Statistics. *Occupational Outlook Handbook, 2006–07.* Available online at http://www.bls.gov/oco

BENIHANA CHEF

Klug, John. *Benihana of Tokyo.* Cambridge, Mass.: Harvard Business School Press, 1998.

Miyuki, Takahashi, and Enami Jouji. *Mr. Benihana: The Rocky Aoki Story.* Tokyo: Mangajin Group, 1997.

BREWMASTER

Daniels, Ray. *Designing Great Beers: The Ultimate Guide to Brewing Classic Beer Styles.* Boulder, Colo.: Brewers Publications, 2000.

Fix, George. *Principles of Brewing Science: A Study of Serious Brewing Issues.* 2nd ed. Boulder, Colo.: Brewers Publications, 2000.

Noonan, Gregory J. *New Brewing Lager Beer: The Most Comprehensive Book for Home and Microbrewers.* Boulder, Colo.: Brewers Publications, 2003.

BUTCHER

Lobel, Stanley, and Leon Evan. *How to Be Your Own Butcher.* New York: Perigee, 1993.

Mettler, John M. *Basic Butchering of Livestock and Game.* North Adams, Mass.: Storey Publishing, LLC, 1986.

Ubaldi, Jack, and Elizabeth Crossman. *Jack Ubaldi's Meat Book: A Butcher's Guide to Buying, Cutting, and Cooking Meat.* New York: Collier Books, 1991.

BUTTERBALL TURKEY TALK-LINE EXPERT

Butterball Turkey Company. *The Butterball Turkey Cookbook.* New York: Hearst Books, 1992.

Daley, Kevin, and Laura Daley-Caravella. *Talk Your Way to the Top: How to Address Any Audience Like Your Career Depends On It.* New York: McGraw-Hill, 2003.

CAKE DECORATOR

Deacon, Carol. *The Complete Step-by-Step Guide to Cake Decorating.* Chanhassen, Minn.: Creative Publishing International, 2003.

Erdosh, George. *Start and Run a Catering Business.* Bellingham, Wash.: Self Counsel Press, 2001.

CHEESE MAKER

Kindsedt, Paul. *American Farmstead Cheese: Complete Guide to Making/Selling Artisan Cheeses.* White River Junction, Vt.: Chelsea Green Publishing Company, 2005.

Lynch, Sarah-Kate. *Blessed Are the Cheesemakers.* New York: Warner Books, 2004.

CHEF-INNKEEPER

Murphy, Martha. *How to Start and Operate Your Own Bed-and-Breakfast: Down-To-Earth Advice from an Award-Winning B&B Owner.* New York: Owl Books, 1994.

Rogak, Lisa Angowski. *Upstart Guide Owning & Managing a Bed & Breakfast.* Chicago: Dearborn Trade, 1994.

CHOCOLATIER

Rosenblum, Mort. *Chocolate: A Bittersweet Saga of Dark and Light.* New York: North Point Press, 2005.

Lebovitz, David. *The Great Book of Chocolate.* Berkeley, Calif.: Ten Speed Press, 2004.

Medrich, Alice. *Bittersweet: Recipes and Tales from a Life in Chocolate.* Muskogee, Okla.: Artisan, 2003.

CIDER MAKER

Proulx, Annie, and Lew Nichols. *Cider: Making, Using and Enjoying Sweet and Hard Cider.* 3rd ed. North Adams, Mass.: Storey Publishing, 2003.

Watson, Ben. *Cider, Hard and Sweet: History, Traditions, and Making Your Own*. Woodstock, Vt.: Countryman Press, 1999.

COFFEE PURVEYOR

Davids, Kenneth. *Coffee: A Guide to Buying, Brewing, and Enjoying*. 5th ed. New York: St. Martin's Griffin, 2001.

Dicum, Gregory, and Nina Luttinger. *The Coffee Book: Anatomy of an Industry from Crop to the Last Drop*. New York: The New Press, 1999.

COOKBOOK AUTHOR

Jacob, Dianne. *Will Write for Food: The Complete Guide to Writing Cookbooks, Restaurant Reviews, Articles, Memoirs, Fiction, and More*. New York: Marlowe and Company, 2005.

Ostmann, Barbara Gibbs, and Jane Baker. *The Recipe Writer's Handbook, Revised & Updated*. Hoboken, N.J.: Wiley, 2001.

Wolfe, Kevin J. *You Can Write a Cookbook*. Cincinnati, Ohio: Writer's Digest Books, 2000.

DAIRY FARMER

Blowey, Roger. *Veterinary Book for Dairy Farmers*. Jackson, Wy.: Farming Press Limited, 1999.

Hughes, Sarah. *My Dad Works on a Farm*. New York: Children's Press, 2000.

Looker, Dan. *Farmers for the Future*. Ames, Iowa: Iowa State Press, 1995.

FISH PURVEYOR

Batchelder, Dorothy. *The Fishmonger Cookbook: From a New England Neighborhood Fish Market – An Expert's Guide to Selecting, Preparing, Cooking and Serving the Very Best Fish*. Emmaus, Pa.: Rodale Press, 1992.

Crother, Cyndi. Catch! *A Fishmonger's Guide to Greatness*. San Francisco: Berrett-Koehler Publishers, 2003.

FAST FOOD FRANCHISEE

Love, John F. *McDonald's: Behind the Arches*. New York: Bantam, 1995.

McDonald, Ronald L. *Ronald McDonald's Franchise Buyers Guide: How to Buy a Fast Food Franchise*. Philadelphia: Xlibris Corp., 1994.

FLAIR BARTENDER

Feller, Robyn M. *The Complete Bartender*. New York: Berkley Publishing Group, 1995.

Regan, Gary. *The Bartender's Bible: 1001 Mixed Drinks and Everything You Need to Know to Set Up Your Bar*. New York: Harper Torch, 1993.

FOOD PACKAGE DESIGNER

Cliff, Stafford. *50 Trade Secrets of Great Design: Packaging*. Gloucester, Mass.: Rockport Publishers, 2002.

Fishel, Catharine. *Design Secrets: Packaging 50 Real-Life Projects Uncovered*. Gloucester, Mass.: Rockport Publishers, 2003.

Roth, Lazlo, and George L. Wybenga. *The Packaging Designer's Book of Patterns*. New York: Wiley, 2000.

FOOD SCULPTOR

Green, B. *The Butter Cow Lady*. Des Moines, Iowa: Target Publishing, 1998.

Friedrich, Julia. *Chocolate Art*. Ostfildern-Ruit, Germany: Cantz Publishing, 2005.

FOOD SERVICE MANAGER

Drummond, Karen Eich, and Lisa M. Brefere. *Nutrition for Foodservice and Culinary Professionals.* New York: Wiley, 2003.

Brown, Douglas Robert. *The Food Service Managers Guide to Creative Cost Cutting and Cost Control.* New York: Atlantic Publishing Company, 2005.

FOOD STYLIST

Carafoli, John, and Rosalind Smith. *Food Photography and Styling: How to Prepare, Light, and Photograph Delectable Food and Drinks.* New York: Watson Guptill Publications, 1992.

Trovato, Rori. *Dishing With Style: Secrets to Great Tastes and Beautiful Presentations.* New York: Clarkson Potter, 2004.

GOURMET FOOD BUSINESS OWNER

Hall, Stephen. *From Kitchen to Market: Selling Your Gourmet Food Specialty.* Dearborn, Mich.: Kaplan Professional, 2000.

Wemischner, Robert, and Karen Karp. *Gourmet to Go: A Guide to Opening and Operating a Specialty Food Store.* New York: Wiley, 1997.

ICE CREAM TASTE TESTER

Arnold, Shannon Jackson. *Everybody Loves Ice Cream: The Whole Scoop on America's Favorite Treat.* Cincinnatti: Emmis Books, 2004.

Older, Jules. *Ice Cream: Including Great Moments in Ice Cream History.* Watertown, Mass.: Charlesbridge Publishing, 2002.

Stogo, Malcolm. *Ice Cream and Frozen Desserts: A Commercial Guide to Production and Marketing.* New York: Wiley, 1997.

ICE SCULPTOR

Amendola, Joseph. *Ice Carving Made Easy.* 2nd ed. Hoboken, N.J.: Wiley, 1994.

Durocher, Joseph F. *Practical Ice Carving.* Boston: CBI Publishing Company, 1981.

Garlough, Robert, Randy Finch, and Derek Maxfield. *Ice Sculpting the Modern Way.* Clifton Park, N.Y.: Thomson Delmar Learning, 2003.

MOVIE SET CATERER

Allen, Judy. *The Business of Event Planning: Behind-the-Scenes Secrets of Successful Special Events.* New York: Wiley, 2002.

Crisafulli, John, Sean Fisher, and Teresa Villa. *Backstage Pass: Catering to Music's Biggest Stars.* Nashville: Cumberland House Publishing, 1998

PASTRY CHEF

Cosgrove, Holli R., ed. "Cooks, Chefs, and Bakers." *Encyclopedia of Careers and Vocational Guidance.* 11th ed. Chicago: Ferguson Publishing Company, 2000.

Donovan, Mary. *Careers for Gourmets and Others Who Relish Food.* Lincolnwood, Ill.: VGM Career Horizons, 1993.

PIZZA MAKER

Boock, Gregory, and Kirk S. Stuart. *Pizza Lover's Cookbook: Creative and Delicious Recipes for Making the World's Favorite Food.* New York: Prima Lifestyles, 1996.

Reinhart, Peter. *American Pie: My Search for the Perfect Pizza.* Berkley, Calif.: Ten Speed Press, 2003.

PRODUCE BUYER

Green, Aliza. *Field Guide to Produce: How to Identify, Select, and Prepare Virtually Every Fruit and Vegetable at the Market.* Philadelphia: Quirk Books, 2004.

Murdich, Jack. *Buying Produce: The Green-grocer's Guide to Selecting and Storing Fresh Fruits and Vegetables.* New York: Hearst Marine Books, 1986.

RESTAURANT REVIEWER
Allen, Gary. *Resource Guide for Food Writers.* New York: Routledge, 1999.

Hughes, Holly. *Best Food Writing 2005.* New York: Marlowe & Company, 2005.

Jacob, Dianne. *Will Write for Food: The Complete Guide to Writing Cookbooks, Restaurant Reviews, Articles, Memoir, Fiction and More.* New York: Marlowe & Company, 2005.

Reichl, Ruth. *Garlic and Sapphires: The Secret Life of a Critic in Disguise.* New York: Penguin Press, 2005.

SCHOOL NUTRITIONIST
Subak-Sharpe, Genell J., and Victor Herbert. *Mount Sinai School of Medicine Complete Book of Nutrition.* New York: St. Martin's Press, 1990.

Wildman, Robert E.C. *The Nutritionist: Food, Nutrition, and Optimal Health.* Binghampton, N.Y.: Haworth Press, 2002.

SOMMELIER
Immer, Andrea. *Great Wine Made Simple: Straight Talk from a Master Sommelier.* New York: Broadway, 2000.

Smith, Brian. *The Sommelier's Guide to Wine: A Primer for Selecting, Serving and Savoring Wine.* New York: Black Dog & Leventhal Publishers, 2003.

SUSHI CHEF
Barber, Kimiko, and Hiroki Takemura. *Sushi: Taste and Techniques.* New York: DK ADULT, 2002.

Maki, Masao. *Spiritual Adventures of a Sushi Chef.* San Francisco: VIZ, LLC, 1997.

Yamamoto, Katsuji, and Roger Hicks. *The Sushi Cookbook: A Step-By-Step Guide to This Popular Japanese Food.* New York: Kodansha America, 1997.

TEST KITCHEN CHEF
Brefere, Lisa M., Karen Eich Drummond, and Brad Barnes. *So You Want to Be a Chef: Your Guide to Culinary Careers.* Hoboken, N.J.: Wiley, 2005.

Dornenburg, Andrew, and Karen Page. *Becoming a Chef.* Hoboken, N.J.: Wiley, 2003.

WINEMAKER (ENOLOGIST)
Boulton, Roger, Vernon Singleton, et. al. *Principles and Practices of Winemaking.* New York: Plenum Press, 1996.

Jackisch, Philip. *Modern Winemaking.* New York: Cornell University Press, 1985.

Vine, Richard P., Ellen Harness, and Sally Linton, eds. *Winemaking: From Grape Growing to Marketplace.* New York: Plenum, 2002.

INDEX

Page numbers in **bold** indicate major treatment of a topic